'In this wise and humane book, psychoanalyst and meditation teacher Jeffrey Rubin shows how the complementary insights of psychoanalysis and Buddhism can be creatively combined in both therapy and daily life. This is a book that will benefit not only therapists—but also everyone seeking to transform legacies of pain and trauma, emerge from self-defeating relational patterns, and live rich, satisfying, and fulfilling lives.'

Seth Zuihō Segall, PhD, *clinical psychologist and Zen Buddhist priest. Contributing editor for Tricycle: The Buddhist Review, science writer for the Mindfulness Research Monthly, and author of Buddhism and Human Flourishing: A Modern Western Perspective (2020)*

'Jeff Rubin has been at the forefront of the conversation between Psychoanalysis and Buddhism for many years. He reviews that conversation with his usual fluent style, thorough scholarship and open hearted personal and clinical candor that will benefit both experienced practitioners and interested newcomers. The book is particularly helpful because Rubin offers actual practice suggestions that bring together Buddhist mindfulness and the best of contemporary psychoanalytic invitations to greater emotional depth and intimacy.'

Mark Finn, PhD, *clinical psychologist and psychoanalyst. Co-editor of Object Relations Theory and Religion (1992) and a contributor to numerous edited collections on Buddhism and psychotherapy, New York*

'This thoughtful, provocative, insightful work illuminates the enormous potential of a genuine marriage between psychoanalytic and Buddhist traditions. Based on decades of experience as a gifted psychoanalyst and diligent meditation student, Dr. Rubin lucidly brings both traditions alive with a clear-eyed understanding of what each offers and lacks. Scholarly yet accessible, and full of relatable personal and clinical examples, this book will enrich the lives and practices of psychotherapists, meditation students, and psychotherapy patients alike.'

Ronald D. Siegel, Psy.D. *Author of The Extraordinary Gift of Being Ordinary: Finding Happiness Right Where You Are, Assistant Professor of Psychology, Part Time, Harvard Medical School*

'Jeffrey Rubin has the courage to look deeply at the intersection of Zen and psychoanalysis – not settling for a simple Venn diagram but asking hard questions about how each wisdom tradition can complement, penetrate, and complete the other. Meditative Psychotherapy and Psychoanalysis will expand your thinking and breathe new life into your work with yourself and others.'

Robert Waldinger, MD, *professor of psychiatry, Harvard Medical School, Roshi, Living Vow Zen*

Meditative Psychotherapy and Psychoanalysis

Jeffrey Rubin's work—the culmination of four decades immersed in psychoanalysis and Eastern mind-body disciplines—introduces a unique method uniting these wisdom traditions. While both aim to alleviate suffering, their attempts at integration often remain superficial. Rubin demonstrates how therapy and meditation compensate for each other's blind spots, providing richer understanding and opening unexpected pathways to healing and transformation.

There's growing interest in blending Eastern meditative and Western psychotherapeutic traditions among practitioners and those seeking deeper self-understanding. In response, Rubin illuminates how these practices, when pursued together, create synergies and offer profound depths of insight impossible to achieve through either discipline alone.

Meditative Psychotherapy and Psychoanalysis provides the conceptual framework underlying the author's *Psychotherapy Case Studies*, offering a comprehensive theoretical foundation that enriches its practical companion volume. Together, these works create a powerful resource for therapists, spiritual seekers, and anyone interested in personal growth, offering a natural path to psychological healing and a more meaningful life.

Jeffrey B. Rubin, PhD, is a psychoanalytically oriented therapist in New York and a Sensei in the Nyogen Senzaki and Soen Nakagawa Zen tradition. He is the author of six books on the integration of Eastern and Western approaches to flourishing and self-transformation. Rubin has taught at various psychoanalytic institutes and meditation, yoga, and growth centers around the country and abroad including the United Nations, Union Theological Seminary, the Esalen Institute, and the 92nd Street Y. His pioneering approach to therapy was featured in *The New York Times* magazine: www.nytimes.com/2009/04/26/magazine/26zen-t.html.

Meditative Psychotherapy and Psychoanalysis

Pathways to Healing and Transformation

Jeffrey B. Rubin

Routledge
Taylor & Francis Group

LONDON AND NEW YORK

Designed cover image: Cavan Images

First published 2026
by Routledge
4 Park Square, Milton Park, Abingdon, Oxon OX14 4RN

and by Routledge
605 Third Avenue, New York, NY 10158

Routledge is an imprint of the Taylor & Francis Group, an informa business

British Library Cataloguing-in-Publication Data
A catalogue record for this book is available from the British Library

ISBN: 978-1-032-98423-0 (hbk)
ISBN: 978-1-032-98297-7 (pbk)
ISBN: 978-1-003-59859-6 (ebk)

DOI: 10.4324/9781003598596

Typeset in Optima
by codeMantra

To my psychoanalytic, Buddhist, yoga, and martial arts teachers: Zvi Lothane, George Atwood, Robert Stolorow, Stephen Mitchell, Monte Ullman, Joseph Goldstein, Jack Kornfield, Christopher Titmuss, Lou Mitsunen Nordstrom, Shinzen Young, Joel Kramer, T.K.V. Desikachar, Dolphi Wertenbaker, Carl Horowitz, Sifu Jeff Jones, Guru Dan Inosanto, Rene Navarro, Edgars Cakuls, Vladimir Vasiliev, Igor Ponizov, Professor Marcio Stambowsky, and Professor Brian Glick with profound gratitude.

I am deeply grateful to the people I have worked with in psychoanalysis and psychotherapy. They have taught me an enormous amount about therapy, healing, and myself. This book—and my life—have been greatly enhanced by our mutual efforts to investigate and understand the depth of their lives.

Contents

Author's Note

This book was written over two decades for different purposes and in different voices—one scholarly and the other more conversational. At times, I have tried to integrate them, which may provide a unified experience for the reader. At other times, I have left them as they originally were which might be disconcerting for some. I'd love it—and I believe it will enhance your experience engaging it—if you were able to greet moments of dissimilar tone with a receptive spirit. This will aid in your understanding of the points I seek to demonstrate about the integration of diverse cultures and sensibilities and a well-lived life.

This book is a work of nonfiction; however, in order to protect the privacy of individuals, names and identifying details have been changed. The experiences, emotions, and themes explored in these pages are authentic and reflect real encounters, although certain details have been modified to respect confidentiality.

Acknowledgments

Writers don't create in isolation. I am blessed to have friends and colleagues who talked through ideas, read chapters—or the whole manuscript—and provided emotional support and vital feedback. Conversations with Diana Alstad, Nicole D'Andria, George Atwood, Mark Banschick, Aileen Blitz, Joe Bobrow, Joanne Cacciatore, John and Suzanne Christopher, Josh Cohen, Paul Cooper, Rick DeBenedetto, Paul Elovitz, Mark Finn, Jefferson Fish, Jerry Garguilo, Uwe Gielen, Skye Goldberg, Suzanne Ironbeiter, Audrey Jacobson, Sifu Jeff Jones, David Kastan, Jesse Kornbluth, Peter Knobler, Joel Kramer, Alexandra Krithades, Lauren Mattia Levine, Henry Lothane, Ellen Luborsky, Aryeh Maidenbaum, John Moody, Lou Mitsunen Nordstrom, Alice Peck, Benito Perry, Ken Porter, Ken Rasmussen, Inna Rozentsvit, Victor Sahn, Lou Salvucci, Tony Stern, Erika Strauss, Mary Traina, Ann Ulanov, Monte Ullman, Marc Wayne, Gail White, Leslie Wolowitz, Richard Wood, and Shinzen Young enriched this manuscript.

I am very appreciative of the invaluable assistance of George Atwood, Alice Peck, Ken Rasmussen, and Inna Rozentsvit, who ensured that the manuscript crossed the finish line.

Kate Hawes, Deepika Batra, Hannah Rayner, Lauren Ellis, Joanna Hardern, and Nandhinee Sekar from Routledge have been a pleasure to work with. Duane Stapp offered invaluable assistance on the cover.

Introduction

There's an explosion of interest in the blending of the Eastern meditative and Western psychotherapeutic traditions among psychotherapists, spiritual seekers, and interested laypeople. We live in a world where increasing numbers of people, including psychoanalysts and psychotherapists, meditate, and in which meditators—including Buddhist teachers—avail themselves of psychoanalysis and psychotherapy. And more young adults are exploring meditation, yoga, and other growth-oriented paths to wellness and healing.

Bringing Buddhism and meditation and psychoanalysis or psychotherapy together no longer seems like a forced marriage. Buddhism is a spiritual system developed 2,500 years ago in India for attaining enlightenment; psychoanalysis is a set of theories and practices that arose in Europe in the late nineteenth century to address psychopathology and mental illness. Buddhism, especially Zen, mistrusts concepts and words and offers a practice that guides individuals as they seek to let go of attachments so as to awaken to a freer sense of self, have a more intimate relationship to the world, and behave with greater ethical wisdom; psychoanalysis uses a self-reflective relationship to explore how formative unconscious experiences from the past shape our sense of self and hidden conflicts in the present.

As we explore further, commonalities—even points of synergy—emerge. Both psychoanalysis and Buddhism are concerned with alleviating suffering and illuminating human identity. Each has a "treatment plan" as well as a diagnosis of what truly afflicts us. And both can help us lessen anguish through cultivating clarity and equanimity, while exploring what it means to be fully human. Each can aid us in more completely inhabiting our lives and experiencing greater intimacy and wisdom. Increasingly, practitioners of each are using—even blending—insights and practices from both, leading to mutual enrichment (e.g. Rubin, 1996, 1999; Finn & Rubin, 2000; Magid, 2002; Engler, 2003; Segall, 2003; Young-Eisendrath, 2003; Aronson, 2004; Unno, 2006; Engler, 2006; Cooper, 2007; Rubin, 2009, 2011; Loizzo, Neale, & Wolf, 2017; Jeon, 2021; Epstein, 2023; Carter, 2023; Cooper, 2023; and Tien, Kawahara, & Davis, 2025). For example, therapists who meditate consistently report that it cultivates greater self-awareness, compassion, and wisdom, and meditation teachers have attested to the value of psychotherapy and psychoanalysis in working on emotional conflicts.

The relationship between the Western psychotherapeutic and Eastern meditative traditions, several decades old, has been a wonderful gift to the world—illuminating the causes of human suffering, as well as offering paths to healing and transformation. The "marriage" of Western psychotherapeutic and Eastern contemplative disciplines promises a drug-free way of addressing painful and stubborn psychological conditions—from anxiety and depression to personality disorders and drug addictions (e.g. Germer & Siegel, 2012). The integration of Western psychological and Asian meditative traditions also provides access to a more meaningful life.

Some years ago, I received an email from a former student, now a contributor to the dialogue between psychoanalysis and Buddhism, who wrote "There's nothing new under the sun to say about psychoanalysis and Buddhism."

"I couldn't disagree with you more," I replied. "We have barely scratched the surface of understanding what they can teach each other and how they can help therapists, their patients, and laypeople alike."

While there is an increasing recognition in the last several decades that the Western psychotherapeutic and Eastern meditative traditions have a great deal to offer each other about lessening human misery and facilitating a psychologically and spiritually healthy life, what's easy to miss, and what almost everyone seems to ignore, is that they are only dating, not emotionally intimate; we have only begun to realize what they can teach each other; and we need to approach them in a new way. Here are three examples: even in recent years, esteemed figures in the field have admitted that their meditative practice is separate from their psychotherapeutic work; or they have only recently begun bringing meditation into therapy; or they graft meditation onto therapy as an adjunctive technique.

The current dialogue between Eastern and Western traditions is haunted by a pervasive tendency to nominally value both but actually venerate and privilege one—usually Buddhism and meditation—while treating the other (typically Western psychotherapy) as a "bridesmaid" who plays second fiddle. I call this lip service to equality and integration *pseudo-complementary*. Authors claim that both psychotherapy and meditation are valuable and express an interest in "integrating" them. But when the chief focus of these efforts is how meditation can help clients and therapists, the value of Western psychotherapeutic theories and practices for Buddhist teachers and students is often neglected. This may be one reason that Buddhism is still plagued by scandals involving teachers sexually exploiting students or illegally expropriating money from their communities (e.g. Boucher, 1988; Rubin, 1996; Kornfield, 2000; Magid, 2002; Engler, 2006; Shaw, 2013; Deveaux, 2017; Remski, 2020; Gleig & Langenberg, 2023), a topic that Western psychology, in general, and psychoanalysis, in particular, can illuminate, which is explored in Chapter 6, "Dancing with Desire: Shining a Psychoanalytic Light on Scandals in Buddhism." For example, psychoanalysis elucidates crucial and sometimes self-harmful self-protective strategies human beings use to heal a damaged sense of self, as well as the psychological appeal of pathological accommodation (Brandchaft, Doctors, & Sorter, 2010), two crucial ingredients in some of these incidents.

The possibility of genuine integration is undermined by the one-sided emphasis on what Buddhism and meditation offer Western psychotherapy.

The second obstacle to a more genuine encounter between the Western psychotherapeutic and Eastern meditative traditions is a tendency to, in the Buddhist sense, be attached to our own cherished theories and practices, and neglect their blind spots. Psychoanalysis can enrich Buddhist understanding of the unconscious psychological obstacles to meditation practice (Rubin, 1996), and Buddhism can aid psychoanalysis in expanding its understanding of greater possibilities for self-transformation. But only if we realize that no one tradition or school of thought has the monopoly on truth or healing, and we are curious about the gaps or omissions in the traditions we most identify with, as well as the potential value of the ones that are outside what we are affiliated with.

In my experience, an authentic dialogue has the following ingredients: awareness of differences, mutual respect, openness and vulnerability, and learning from one another. And these ingredients should be part of the conversation between Buddhists and psychoanalysts or psychotherapists.

A sign that this is happening—that there is what I call a "close encounter of a new kind" (Rubin, 1999) between the Western psychotherapeutic and Eastern meditative disciplines—is that both traditions are sometimes surprised and enriched by their encounter with each other (Rubin, 1999). Rarely does that happen. Too often there is what Freud (1927), in *The Future of an Illusion*, called a "monologue without interruption," a one-sided exchange in which neither side is really touched, changed, or transformed by an encounter. I witnessed this first-hand as a participant in a conference called "Healing the Suffering Self: A Dialogue Among Psychoanalysts and Buddhists" held in 1994 at the Harvard Club in New York City. Prominent psychoanalysts and Buddhists presented papers. As I attended the presentations and conversed with many of the participants, it was evident that not only was there little dialogue between representatives of each tradition, but also they did not seem altered in any perceivable way by the encounter with the other. That pattern has been repeated in subsequent conferences I have participated in since then. When that happens something vital is missing.

Why do psychoanalysis and meditation need each other? Therapy and meditation not only compensate for the other's blind spots, but also, when practiced together, can provide a richer understanding than either discipline pursued alone.

My own experiences over four decades with meditation and psychoanalysis have led me to create what I call *meditative psychoanalysis*, an integrative model which blends the best aspects of Western psychoanalysis and Eastern meditative traditions into a more encompassing synthesis. In meditative analysis, therapist and patient first use meditation and yogic breathing or any genuine awareness practice (from qigong to T'ai Chi) to cultivate heightened focus and attentiveness, and then explore and translate the meaning of what they have discovered using psychoanalytic understandings of symbolic and unconscious communication. Psychoanalytic attention to hidden meaning and understanding—the second facet of meditative psychoanalysis—expands the concentration and equanimity that meditation by itself fosters. The third and final aspect of meditative psychoanalysis is a special relationship (and environment) designed to illuminate and transform one's history. Psychoanalysis not only elucidates the interpersonal roots of adult afflictions, but it also offers a relationship and experience that is a vehicle for transformation in the present. In tandem with meditation, the therapeutic relationship—seen in a freer, more empathic, and creative light—becomes a crucible in which recurrent patterns of restrictively seeing and organizing one's life can be witnessed and ultimately transformed, so that new and liberating kinds of human connections can occur.

What's unique about this model is that it provides a concrete and accessible way of integrating Asian contemplative and Western psychotherapeutic and psychoanalytic traditions in practice. The artful blending of mindful presence and psychological insight in the context of an emotionally intimate relationship, that is, a sacred connection, can facilitate genuine transformation and authentic healing.

I'll illustrate my theoretical reflections with examples from my practice, which, like the clinical stories in *Psychotherapy Case Studies* (Rubin, 2025), make the concepts more accessible and give the reader a felt sense of my perspective. Writings on psychotherapy and Buddhism often lack sustained illustrative material that fleshes out how the therapist actually blends psychotherapy and meditation or challenges the author's assumptions and point of view, which is crucial for testing theoretical assumptions and refining the dialogue between psychotherapy or psychoanalysis and Buddhism.

The second section of the book provides examples of meditative psychoanalysis from a psychoanalytic treatment with a Zen master to a psychoanalytic exploration of scandals in Buddhism. The section concludes with a chapter that illuminates how we can deepen our own meditative training as well as practice meditative psychotherapy.

The third section takes meditative psychoanalysis out of the office and into the world with chapters on the interferences to love and the psychology of hate and transience and a well-lived life.

The concluding section offers resources for theoretical study of Buddhism and meditation and psychoanalysis, as well as continuing and deepening one's meditative practice.

When I teach or supervise psychoanalysts or psychotherapists I often say, "It's all in the listening."

References

Aronson, Harvey. *Buddhist Practice on Western Ground: Reconciling Eastern Ideals and Western Psychology*. Boston, MA: Shambhala Publications, 2004.

Boucher, Sandy. *Turning the Wheel: American Women Creating the New Buddhism*. San Francisco: Harper & Row, 1988.

Brandchaft, Bernard, Shelley Doctors, and Dorienne Sorter. *Toward an Emancipatory Psychoanalysis: Brandchaft's Intersubjective Vision*. London: Routledge, 2010.

Carter, Helen. *Weaving the Paths of Buddhism and Psychotherapy: The Practice of Human Being*. London: Routledge, 2023.

Cooper, Paul, ed. *Into the Mountain Stream: Psychotherapy and Buddhist Experience*. Lanham, MD: Jason Aronson, 2007.

Cooper, Paul. *Psychoanalysis and Zen Buddhism*. London: Routledge, 2023.

Deveaux, Tynette. "Kagyu Thubten Choling (Now Palpung Thubten Choling) Addresses Sangha about Lama Norlha Rinpoche's Sexual Misconduct with Students." *Lion's Roar*, July 15, 2017.

Engler, Jack. "Being Somebody and Being Nobody: A Reexamination of the Understanding of Self in Psychoanalysis and Buddhism." In *Psychoanalysis and Buddhism: An Unfolding Dialogue*, edited by Jeremy Safran. Boston, MA: Wisdom Publications, 2003. Pages 35–79.

Engler, Jack. "Promises and Perils on the Spiritual Path." In *Buddhism and Psychotherapy Across Cultures: Essays on Theories and Practices*, edited by Mark Unno. Boston, MA: Wisdom Publications, 2006. Pages 17–30.

Epstein, Mark. *The Zen of Therapy: Uncovering a Hidden Kindness in Life*. New York: Penguin, 2023.

Finn, Mark, and Jeffrey Rubin. "Psychotherapy with Buddhists." In *Handbook of Psychotherapy and Religious Diversity*, edited by P. Scott Richards and Allen Bergin. Washington, DC: American Psychological Association, 2000. Pages 317–340.

Freud, Sigmund. *The Future of an Illusion*. Standard Edition, 21. London: Hogarth Press, 1927. Pages 3–56.

Germer, Christopher, and Ronald Siegel, eds. *Wisdom and Compassion: Deepening Mindfulness in Clinical Practice*. New York: Guilford Press, 2012.

Gleig, Ann, and Amy Langenberg. "Sexual Ethics and Healthy Boundaries in the Wake of Teacher Abuse." *Buddhadharma: The Practitioner's Quarterly*, December 5, 2023.

Jeon, Hyunsoo. *Buddhist Psychotherapy: Wisdom from Early Buddhist Teaching*. New York: Springer, 2021.

Kornfield, Jack. *After the Ecstasy, the Laundry*. New York: Bantam Books, 2000.

Loizzo, Joseph, Neale, Miles, and Wolf, Emily, eds. *Advances in Contemplative Therapy: Accelerating Healing and Transformation*. London: Routledge, 2017.

Magid, Barry. *Ordinary Mind: Exploring the Common Ground of Zen and Psychotherapy*. Boston, MA: Wisdom Publications, 2002.

Remski, Matthew. "Survivors of an International Buddhist Cult Share Their Stories." *The Walrus*, September 28, 2020.

Rubin, Jeffrey B. *Psychotherapy and Buddhism: Toward an Integration*. New York: Plenum, 1996.

Rubin, Jeffrey B. "Close Encounters of a New Kind: Toward an Integration of Psychoanalysis and Buddhism." *The American Journal of Psychoanalysis* 59, no. 1 (1999): 5–24.

Rubin, Jeffrey B. "Deepening Psychoanalytic Listening: The Marriage of Buddha and Freud." *The American Journal of Psychoanalysis* 69 (2009): 93–105.

Rubin, Jeffrey B. *The Art of Flourishing: A New East-West Approach to Staying Sane and Finding Love in an Insane World*. New York: Crown, 2011.

Rubin, Jeffrey B. *Psychotherapy Case Studies: Escaping the Prison You Didn't Know You Were In*. London: Routledge, 2025.

Segall, Seth. *Encountering Buddhism: Western Psychology and Buddhist Teachings*. Albany, NY: SUNY Press, 2003.

Shaw, Daniel. *Traumatic Narcissism: Relational Systems of Subjugation*. London: Routledge, 2013.

Tien, Liang, Kawahara, Debra, and Davis, Erin. *Buddhist Psychotherapy: Connecting Early Buddhism to Mindfulness and Western Psychotherapy*. Washington, DC: American Psychological Association, 2025.

Unno, Mark, ed. *Buddhism and Psychotherapy Across Cultures: Essays on Theories and Practices*. Boston, MA: Wisdom Publications, 2006.

Young-Eisendrath, Polly. "Transference and Transformation in Buddhism and Psychoanalysis." In *Psychoanalysis and Buddhism: An Unfolding Dialogue*, edited by Jeremy Safran. Boston, MA: Wisdom Publications, 2003. Pages 301–318.

Part I
Meditative Psychoanalysis

1   The Roots of Meditative Psychotherapy and Psychoanalysis

Meditative psychoanalysis developed over time and in several stages linked to its three components—heightened attentiveness to mind and body; understanding of unconscious meaning; and emotional intimacy, creativity, and playfulness.

Confusion and emotional pain can be bewildering and demoralizing. It can also spur a passionate quest for self-understanding and a fervent wish to comprehend the source of the distress. My family—and the subtle but significant madness-posing-as-sanity that permeated my childhood—caused me to become an ardent psychological detective; someone who was inspired to unravel emotional mysteries—including what was going on beneath the manicured surface that was my family. Great literature—Sophocles and Shakespeare, Melville and Toni Morrison—were my first allies in untangling the conundrums of childhood. Later, psychoanalysis and Eastern meditative disciplines deepened my efforts. Both transformed my understanding of listening, the first ingredient of meditative psychoanalysis.

Listening and Heightened Attentiveness

While listening is easy to describe and sounds simple to do, it's actually complex and trainable. My first realization of this occurred in 1980 when I was at a professional crossroads in my life: I wasn't sure whether I should stay in New York and study psychoanalysis or move to California, get a PhD in East-West studies, and study yoga with a remarkable man named Joel Kramer, a pioneer and legend of modern American yoga, who some consider its founding father. Talking about this conflict in my own psychoanalysis was not clarifying. After a weekend yoga workshop with Joel Kramer in New York City, we took a long walk in Central Park. As I described my conflict and confusion, he listened with an extraordinary attentiveness and undivided concentration that I had never experienced. He was fully engaged in what I was saying without any presuppositions, preferences, or biases. He was not hunting for confirmation of what he believed or desired. All that existed was what I was grappling with.

His response surprised me: "I think that you need to stay in New York and study psychoanalysis." His agenda-less listening has served as a touchstone

DOI: 10.4324/9781003598596-2

and an inspiration and planted a seed that became a crucial facet of meditative psychoanalysis.

Joel gave me a second, related gift that was indispensable in cultivating listening and creating meditative psychoanalysis—namely a radically new methodology for self-investigation which he learned from the
twentieth-century Indian philosopher Jiddu Krishnamurti. Joel describes his
approach in an interview with Jeanne Malmgren Cameron entitled "Mind
in Asana" (1986):

> an inward turning of the mind onto itself… a quality of awareness in
> which the mind turns in upon itself and begins to observe its own con-
> ditioning process. You're not saying, 'Oh, I shouldn't be doing this,'
> you're not necessarily trying to control it or make it go away, you're
> just becoming interested in the nature of mental conditioning…[It's] a
> quality of awareness that does nothing but observe. You observe the
> movement of thought within yourself; you don't try to silence it or make
> it go away. You're trying to catch it in the moment of its appearance…
> Although it sounds simple, this is probably one of the most difficult
> things to do, because it's very hard to do nothing and just take a look at
> what's happening. But this, I feel, is how we move toward real under-
> standing. Growth almost always involves a shattering of self-images, a
> major shift in one's habitual life patterns.

"I began to see," Kramer adds,

> how the mind structures and conditions. How it builds habits, and
> how those habits actually filter our perception of the world. I began to
> observe how I dodge things with my mind, how I separate myself from
> others out of fear or out of a need to feel better than they…Much of the
> structure of our conditioning reveals itself only in our relationships. Let's
> say, for example, that you and I have a relationship. If you hurt my feel-
> ings, I'll start to see you through the filter or memory of that hurt. There
> are lots of things I could do with that: I could forgive you, I could avoid
> you, I could ignore you, or I could eke out a little vengeance against
> you—not necessarily even consciously—by a sharp word or a subtle
> put-down, or by telling my friends what a drag you are. And I would
> probably enjoy this vengeance, even though I don't acknowledge that
> I'm a vengeful person. But if I begin to look closely at the nature of this
> relationship, I can observe that when you hurt me, I automatically want
> to hurt back. If I can just observe this automatic, conditioned response
> without judging it, I can see my conditioning. And that seeing frees
> me from having to react to you in an automatic way. In order to do
> that, though, I have to be willing to look. Many traditions touch on
> this—Vipassana, certain Hindu techniques, Taoist traditions. They're all
> describing a quality of awareness that does nothing but observe.

Ongoing self-reflection is crucial for self-transformation as well as meditative psychoanalysis. It leads to a capacity in the moment to see, adapt, and change, which fosters on-going personal growth and evolution.

There's a venerable—and perhaps neglected—tradition of self-examination in psychoanalysis called self-analysis. Venerable because it was begun by Freud, crucial to his self-understanding and the creation of psychoanalytic insights and theories; and continued by Jung and Ferenczi, Winnicott and Kohut, Klein and Bion, Searles and Racker, Jacobs and Silverman, and their successors. But this tradition is also somewhat overlooked, which is why the story of Erich Fromm devoting "a daily hour to self-analysis" (Mitchell, 1993) is both inspiring and seemingly atypical.

Self-analysis, like listening, is more complex than it might initially appear. A crucial challenge is *countertransference*—it is difficult to see what we can't (and most need to) see about ourselves. Analysts of earlier decades viewed countertransference as "both avoidable and regrettable" (Mitchell, 1993).

The notion of countertransference has undergone a sea-change in psychoanalysis—from Freud's (1910) view that it was due to the patient's influence and was a personal problem for the analyst, to contemporary classical and relationally oriented perspectives emphasizing its potential value— especially the way it may bring to the surface key elements of one's buried, disavowed history and can shed light on internal and interpersonal challenges of the analyst and the analysand.

I assumed countertransference was the key obstacle to self-investigation until I first encountered Joel's perspective. Something clicked on a profound level when I was first heard his emphasis on non-judgmental self-observation: his simple-sounding description resonated and gave me a glimpse of new vistas in a way that normal discussions of self-examination and self-reflection didn't. The process he described felt more direct, visceral, and emotional than the usual recourse in self-analysis to more intellectualized, impersonal, and psychologically-detached formulations. In other words, in my experience—and yours might be different—whether it was Freud looking for oedipal dynamics in himself or Searles assuming that his private reactions and feelings to his patient reflected the patient's unconscious dynamics that were being conveyed to him; we mental health professionals all-too-often *listen for what we know or believe* instead of *listening to what is happening*. Joel and Krishnamurti's methodology of unmediated self-examination helped me experience the latter.

Listening to the Body

In "Recommendations to Physicians Practising Psycho-Analysis" Sigmund Freud famously and evocatively wrote about listening in his technical recommendations that

> the analyst must turn his own unconscious like a receptive organ towards the transmitting unconscious of the patient. He must adjust

himself to the patient as a telephone receiver is adjusted to the transmitting microphone. Just as the receiver converts back into sound waves the electric oscillations in the telephone line which were set up by sound waves, so the doctor's unconscious is able, from the derivatives of the unconscious which are communicated to him, to reconstruct that unconscious, which has determined the patient's free association.

Joel's non-judgmental self-observation and Freud's decoding of unconscious messages were both crucial to the development of listening and meditative psychoanalysis. As was Eastern somatic practices.

For several decades, Eastern contemplative practices—from Buddhist meditation to Indian yoga—have been an important part of my life on a personal and professional level. In recent years, I have also become extremely interested in internal Chinese somatic practices like Chi Kung (or qigong), Chinese for "energy mastery," a corporal art and physical discipline involving deliberate movement, relaxed breathing, and mental focus that strengthens immunity and expands internal attentiveness. Intensive daily practice has measurably deepened somatic sensitivity and awareness. It has also broadened my view of listening.

"Mr. Duffy lived a short distance from his body," James Joyce wrote in *Dubliners*. We need to listen to the body. Most people don't.

While Freud's "early path-breaking work [in *Studies on Hysteria*] was grounded in an active engagement with his clients' bodies… 'pressing,' and 'kneading' a patient's legs… and holding patients' heads with his hands to help them access memories" (Totton, 2020), the body has been relatively neglected in his work and by subsequent analysts. There is a tradition in psychoanalysis and psychotherapy of attending to the body (e.g. Ferenczi, 1929/1955; Reich, 1942; Perls, Hefferline, & Goodman, 1951; Lowen, 1976; Kurtz, 1985; Levine, 1997; Ogden, Minton, & Paine, 2006; and Totton, 2020). And contemporary relationally and bodily oriented therapists recognize that therapy occurs as a living intersection of two people with bodies and minds. But attunement to our own bodies as a source of embodied knowledge and wisdom in the treatment seems somewhat overlooked and under-developed. Meditative psychoanalysis attempts to integrate what Totton (2020), in a felicitous phrase, terms a *visceral* and a *visual* perspective—attending to the *therapist's corporal experience*, as well as the *analysand's bodily movements and physical symptoms*.

When we are attuned to the body a whole other world opens up—we notice subtle and fleeting somatic sensations and visual images and that deeply enriches our capacity to listen and comprehend. And this has played a crucial role in the creation and practice of meditative psychoanalysis.

My own approach was to take Joel and Krishnamurti's method of self-examination and Freud's interest in unconscious communication and integrate them with a more explicit emphasis on the body and emotional experiences, which cultivated the first foundation of meditative psychoanalysis, heightened attentiveness.

What I realized some years ago—and this, for me, was a game-changer—was that meditation is wonderful at fostering enhanced focus, but it neglects a crucial facet of listening: discovering meaning and fostering understanding, which are hallmarks of psychoanalysis.

Understanding

The world is permeated by pain. In the face of so much sadism and stunning heartlessness, it is natural and inevitable that we shut down and take short cuts. Psychotherapeutic healing, however, goes in a different direction. In Dante's *Divine Comedy*, the Roman poet Virgil accompanies Dante into hell. In our speedy, immediate-gratification-oriented, and pain-averse world, no one wants to be Virgil anymore—to go into hell with Dante. But the willingness to explore with patience and empathy the actual experience of what people undergo, no matter how horrific, is indispensable in responding to the emotional afflictions that haunt human beings. And we shouldn't be surprised that recipients of such understanding will be capable of both remarkable resilience and extraordinary healing.

I was exceptionally fortunate to experience this first-hand with a devoted and gifted psychoanalyst, who was willing to accompany me into the hellish world that was my family. This not only freed me from the prison I didn't know I was in; it provided an inspiring vision of a very different way of conceiving of the psychotherapeutic journey and relationship—the analyst as jazz improviser, grounded in the fundamentals of human development and the therapeutic process, yet able to adapt and evolve based on the exigencies of the moment. Combined with agenda-less listening and non-judgmental self-observation of mind, body, and emotions, this formed the three pillars of meditative psychoanalysis: heightened attentiveness, understanding of unconscious communication and meaning, and emotional intimacy.

Zen supplemented and expanded all of this—pointing to a vision of greater emotional connectedness, creativity, and playfulness in everyday life, as well as a practice to integrate these three facets of meditative psychoanalysis (listening, understanding, and emotional intimacy and creativity) into one's ordinary existence-—including psychotherapy.

Zen and Emotional Intimacy

"You know, you're a Zen guy," my patient, a Zen master, said to me as he was leaving our first session years ago.

It took some time for me to realize what he meant, and when I did, the final crucial aspect of meditative psychoanalysis emerged.

"What is Zen?" a bull-in-the-china-shop, middle-aged accountant once asked me as I passed by the table he was sitting at as I was leaving the gym.

"It was developed many centuries ago in China…" I began, in a remarkably un-Zen like answer.

"Gimme the short version," he shot back.

"Did you have coffee this morning?" I asked.

"Yeah." He raised his Styrofoam cup.

"Did you really taste it, or were you a million miles away?"

"I really tasted it."

"That's Zen," I said.

"Okay, I can go with that."

"Zen is teaching adults what comes naturally to children," I added as I left the gym.

In an ideal world, Zen wouldn't be necessary. Adults wouldn't need to be reminded to wake up and innocently and whole-heartedly appreciate the song of the birds or the smell of the lilacs. It would come naturally, as it does for most children.

But most of us do need to be reminded, and Zen—a meditative awareness practice that cultivates un-self-consciousness and spontaneous responsiveness—is necessary. One of the first—and most momentous—insights of Buddhist practice (regardless of what type of meditation) is how asleep we are.

Without sustained practice we sleepwalk through the only life we have; self-absorbed and inattentive, encased in our own private and insular universe, missing the moment, and alienated from the world...and ourselves.

One of the crucial reasons adults have to be reminded to "Be Here Now" is because of the nature of existence in the twenty-first century. The pace of existence is accelerated and merciless. The digital revolution and the recent technologies have miraculously linked us to an ever-expanding network of people, places, and products. But we are relentlessly "on call" via cell phones and texting, voice messages, and emails. We not only juggle back-breaking demands, but we are also bombarded and assaulted with more information than we can possibly digest—much of it trivial and fiercely addictive. Given the alluring array of diversions—think of them as Weapons of Mass Distraction—from Tik Tok to Instagram, it is not surprising that we are not only inattentive and depleted but training a collective—and ever-growing—attention-deficit disorder (Rubin, 2011).

The second reason adults have so much trouble being present lies in the nature of human development.

The Adult Fall or Innocence and Passion Lost

"Grow up. Stop being so immature and childish," I overhear an exasperated mother saying to her son in the park. He is all over the place, rolling in the grass, chewing on God-knows-what, laughing hysterically, chasing after butterflies—or playing tag with imaginary companions? At first the frustrated mother's remarks seem reasonable. We can all empathize with her annoyance. Many of us have said—or thought—similar things. Her son is exhausting to be with and may, at times, do things that endanger his health—what exactly does he have in his mouth?

Growing up and developing the ability to use language in ever more sophisticated ways, letting go of childish preoccupations, and becoming more "mature"—is a good thing. *Right?*

The question is: Has anything been sacrificed?

Consider for a moment what happens when a person actually "grows-up" and becomes an adult. Childhood is often a state of grace in which almost everything is new—and full of wonder. Children see with fresh eyes unclouded by the preconceptions, beliefs, and social conventions characterizing—and alienating—adults. Experiences are more innocently and directly experienced by children, rather than slotted into the conceptual categories and boxes that adults use to simplify life. Adult perceptions are filtered through sophisticated language, which often bleaches out and obscures the richness and texture of what we are experiencing. An adult who is observing cars slowing down and gawking at an accident calls it "rubbernecking;" a child I know, unhampered by adult language, evocatively described the same phenomena with the less generic and more descriptive "turtle-necking."

Adults look but often don't see; listen and frequently don't hear; eat and don't taste. Children often revel in what harried adults rush past. Most adults abandon or dampen child-like wonderment and the passion it often gives birth to, so that the "business" or "work" of adulthood can get under way. They fall victim to what Karen Horney (1950) terms the "tyranny of the should"—enslaved by what they think they are supposed to do—rather than what they are passionate about. Most adults are in a huge hurry to be practical, competent, and responsible. They want to earn a living, succeed at work, find a mate, and raise a family and often treat imagination and exuberance as signs of immaturity, of an unwillingness to 'grow up,' an inability to 'take life seriously,' instead of part of the vitality of a lively and passionate life. Following your dreams, for all-too-many adults, seems silly, unrealistic, and a waste of time.

Becoming an adult has within it a secret cost that few people consider—an "adult fall"—a loss of the innocence and un-self-consciousness of childhood when life was experienced directly and intimately without the filters and distance that adults take for granted. While we are programmed to believe that the movement from the pre-reflective, un-self-conscious state of childhood to the reflective consciousness of adulthood is a fortunate progression; Zen, like Taoism, recognizes that pre-reflective, un-self-consciousness is deeply valuable and shouldn't be replaced (Nordstrom, personal communication, March 27, 2009). The world, for children, is animated and miraculous. Growing up, for most adults means growing away from the authenticity, aliveness, and passion of our childhood. Adults become unnatural and alienated from direct experience, themselves, and other people; and are unaware of it. And they often believe that their preoccupied, detached state is all there is—and they are complacent about it. But the un-self-consciousness and spontaneity we forsake as we become responsible and mature may contribute to an unconscious melancholy that permeates the lives of many adults.

"Is there a cure for self-alienation?" a brilliant and very alienated young adult asked me years ago.

"Zen," I replied. Direct and enigmatic, profound and embarrassingly simple, Zen, a school of Buddhism originating in China in 520 CE, like other Buddhist traditions including Tibetan, Chan, and Vipassana, has taken root in American culture in the last several decades. No longer the province of Beat poets, artists, and counter-cultural types, Zen influences how we work and play sports, parent and love. *And how we practice therapy.*

Students of Zen attest to its life-changing impact. But it's often difficult to pinpoint exactly what it is. Zen eludes our efforts to define it or put it into a formula or sound bite. It is simple, but not easy, unless you are a child—or an adult who hasn't lost her un-self-conscious youthful innocence. Aware that the "gates of Eden are not locked"—adults can access child-like innocence now (Nordstrom, personal communication, March 29, 2009)—Zen is suspicious of verbal descriptions and conceptualizations and notoriously resistant to categorization.

And stating what Zen is—like offering a prose summary of a great poem—not only misses the point, but it also betrays the spirit of Zen. Books about Zen and Zen centers abound, often obscuring its marrow, but authentic Zen, immediate and unadorned—a flash of lightning through the summer sky—is rarer.

A woman told Shunryu Suzuki, author of the classic *Zen Mind, Beginner's Mind*, that she found it difficult to mix Zen practice with the demands of being a stay-at-home spouse. "I feel I'm trying to climb a ladder. But for every step upward, I slip backward two steps."

"Forget the ladder," Suzuki told her. "In Zen everything is right here on the ground" (Chadwick, 2001).

Zen is intimacy—no separation—between the experiencer and the experience. "Be deluded," one of my Zen teacher's teachers said to him; by which I think he meant, whole-heartedly be that. Or joy, sadness, or whatever we are experiencing.

Zen thrives in the ordinary miracles we often take-for-granted, rather than rarefied ideas. A psychiatrist asked Suzuki about the nature of consciousness.

"I just try to teach my students how to hear the birds sing," he replied (Chadwick, 2001).

Zen serves life—rather than the other way around. A student told Suzuki about a powerful experience in which he felt amazing spaciousness.

"Yes, you could call that enlightenment," Suzuki said, "but it's best to forget about it. And how's your work coming?" (Chadwick, 2001).

Zen is taking care of business: Suzuki and his students took some tools and walked up a hot, dusty trail to work on a project. When they got to the top, they discovered that they had forgotten a shovel, and the students began a discussion about who should get it. After the discussion had ended, they realized that Suzuki wasn't there. He was already halfway down the mountain trail, on his way to pick up the shovel (Chadwick, 2001).

Zen is inclusive. Suzuki bought old vegetables from an old woman at a grocery near the San Francisco Zen Center. One day the woman said, "Here are some fresh ones. Why don't you take them?"

"The fresh ones will be bought anyway," he said (Chadwick, 2001).

We need Zen so that we can be better hosts—a welcoming spirit to what we encounter. Zen helps us be intimate with what we meet and un-self-consciously and spontaneously respond to life—and ourselves.

Freud's (1912) recommendation that therapists "free associate"—which we might conceive of as an unfettered mind and consciousness playing and roaming unimpededly—enriched Zen's emphasis on intensified connectedness and emotional intimacy.

Zen and psychoanalysis were of inestimable aid in helping me engage my life—and my work—more fully and wholeheartedly, creatively and playfully. And that was the third and final facet of meditative psychoanalysis.

References

Chadwick, David. *Zen Is Right Here: Teaching Stories and Anecdotes of Shunryu Suzuki*. Boston: Shambhala, 2001.

Ferenczi, Sandor. "The Principle of Relaxation and Neocatharsis." In *Final Contributions to the Problems and Methods of Psychoanalysis*, edited by Michael Balint. New York: Brunner/Mazel, 1929/1955. Pages 108–125.

Freud, Sigmund. "The Future Prospects of Psycho-Analytic Therapy." *Standard Edition* 11. London: Hogarth Press, 1910. Pages 139–151.

Freud, Sigmund. "Recommendations to Physicians Practising Psycho-Analysis." *Standard Edition* 12. London: Hogarth Press, 1912. Pages 109–120.

Horney, Karen. "The Tyranny of the Should." In *Neurosis and Human Growth*. New York: W. W. Norton & Company, 1950. Page 65, 64–85.

Kurtz, Ron. *Hakomi Therapy*. Second Edition. San Francisco, CA: Hakomi Institute, 1985.

Levine, Peter. *Waking the Tiger: Healing Trauma*. Berkeley, CA: North Atlantic Books, 1997.

Lowen, Alexander. *Bioenergetics*. New York: Penguin, 1976.

Mitchell, Stephen. "Foreword." In *Self-Analysis: Critical Inquiries, Personal Vistas*, edited by James Barron. Hillsdale, NJ: The Analytic Press, 1993. Page xv, xvii.

Ogden, Pat, Kekuni Minton, and Clare Paine. *Trauma and the Body: A Sensorimotor Approach to Psychotherapy*. New York: W.W. Norton, 2006.

Perls, Fritz, Ralph Hefferline, and Paul Goodman. *Gestalt Therapy: Excitement and Growth in the Human Personality*. New York: Julian Press, 1951.

Reich, Wilhelm. *The Discovery of the Orgone: The Function of the Orgasm*. New York: The Noonday Press, 1942.

Rubin, Jeffrey B. *The Art of Flourishing: A New East-West Approach to Staying Sane and Finding Love in an Insane World*. New York: Random House, 2011.

Totton, Nick. *Body Psychotherapy for the 21st Century*. London: Karnac Books, 2020. Pages 26–27.

2 Deepening Listening
The Marriage of Buddha and Freud

Meditative psychoanalysis has three components: *listening, understanding, and liberated intimacy*. Let's begin with the first element—listening.

"My, the lights are bright in here," a client said to me in her first session many years ago.

I wondered, where are lights bright?

As she discussed what brought her to therapy and what she was struggling with in her life—a feeling of self-contempt and never being "good-enough"—I listened on two channels, focusing on what she was consciously saying and on her suggestive image.

Lights are bright in a police station, I eventually thought to myself. When I asked her if coming to therapy made her feel "grilled under the lights by the cops," she smiled nervously and told me about her fears of being judged in therapy. Since she always judged herself, she assumed that a stranger would have to judge her. After my question, she noticeably relaxed and spoke more freely and openly.

Listening is an essential component of the psychotherapeutic process. It is indispensable to all that the therapist does, whether a psychoanalyst, dialectical-behavioral therapist, or a trauma and body-oriented clinician. In each case, careful listening aids the therapist in decoding the client's unconscious communications and empathetically understanding their life. An equally important aspect of listening is the therapist's awareness of their own internal emotional and physical reactions. Are we suppressing irritation, sadness, or hopelessness with a patient who is stuck? Are we feeling connected and relaxed or is our body tightening? In addition, therapeutic listening is infinitely enhanced when the therapist can access their own imaginative capacities. Are we aware of subtle, but potentially significant, feelings or images, fantasies or somatic sensations? Might any of this shed light on the patient or the therapeutic process?

"In all our vast [therapeutic] literature," notes Coltart (1992), "very little attention has been paid to attention." Despite the importance of listening, we take it for granted, and it is rarely discussed.

Freud (1912) identified the ideal state of mind for therapists when they listen—what he called "evenly hovering" or "evenly suspended attention."

DOI: 10.4324/9781003598596-3

This is a state in which the therapist is alert and receptive and grounded and flexible. Listening in this manner helps the therapist attend to both what the patient is saying—or not saying—and how the therapist is reacting. Without "evenly hovering attention," the therapist, writes Freud (1912), "is in danger of never finding anything but what he already knows." When one listens with "evenly hovering attention," a whole new universe opens up as patient and therapist become aware of hidden thoughts and feelings, fantasies and bodily sensations, which enables them to understand themselves and live more freely.

Freud gave mental health professionals a profound gift—a discovery that has never been superseded. No one in the therapeutic literature has amended or revised his seminal recommendations. Yet, neither Freud nor his contemporaries or successors who explored this territory (e.g. Ferenczi, Horney, Fromm, Bion, and Langs) offered positive recommendations for how to cultivate this crucial yet eminently trainable state of mind. Freud and Bion, for example, focused on the obstructions to facilitating it—what not to do (Rubin, 1996). The former indicated that the analyst should neither try too hard to prematurely figure out the meaning of the patient's communications—a state of mind he called "reflection"—nor should the analyst attempt to formulate or write about a case prematurely. Bion (1970) encouraged therapists to listen without "memory, desire or understanding"—that is, without preconceptions about who the client is or expectations for what should happen in the treatment.

The fact that no one in the psychotherapeutic literature has formulated how one actually cultivates "evenly hovering attention" leaves an important gap in therapy training and technique—one that has never been filled—but perhaps a tradition outside psychoanalysis can be of assistance. If therapists were trained to really listen with evenly hovering attention to each client, not only would the clinical data more readily challenge and expand their own most cherished formulations, but they would find it more difficult to maintain allegiance to single schools of psychotherapeutic thought. And our understanding of our own counter-transference—those emotional factors that interfere with our capacity to empathize with and help our clients—would be enhanced.

Try this experiment:

1 Close your eyes, sit still, and try to notice how you are feeling emotionally and physically.
2 Open your eyes and write down what you perceived.

Now, try another experiment:

1 Close your eyes. Since you are going to be breathing through the nose, please close your mouth. Breathe without straining. Begin with a long exhalation, gently pressing your abdomen toward your spine. Do this for twelve quiet and easeful breaths.

2 Now take a long exhalation, gently pressing your abdomen toward your spine, and try, as best you can, to make each exhalation slightly longer than each inhalation, without straining. Do this for twelve breaths.
3 Notice any places of tranquility in your body. Feel and appreciate them. Do this for several minutes.
4 Open your eyes and return your attention to the room.
5 Write down what you noticed.

When I did this exercise during a course I was teaching at a psychoanalytic institute on psychoanalytic listening, the psychoanalysts-in-training reported that after they tried to determine how they were feeling before doing pranayama, yogic breathing, and meditating, they thought they were relaxed and aware, but after meditating they realized how unaware they had been. They also recognized that meditating helped them tune in to what they were feeling emotionally and physically to a much greater extent than self-observation alone.

Coltart (1992) claims that the practice of paying attention is the same whether taught by a Buddhist meditation master or an experienced analyst. But they are actually very different.

Psychoanalysis lacks an appreciation for cultivating two qualities that meditation fosters, namely concentration and equanimity. These are heightened states of focus and acceptance that are not even mapped in Western psychologies. Explaining the meditative process in some detail—what it is and how to do it—will illuminate this.

Misunderstandings about meditation abound. It has been viewed as everything from a "self-improvement technique" to a "passive withdrawal from the world" (Welwood, 2000). "Meditation" is not one thing such as a technique to lower stress or blood pressure or quiet the mind. There are many kinds of meditation including Christian, Catholic, Jewish, Sufi, Taoist, Yogic, Hindu, and Buddhist types. Goleman's (1988) *The Meditative Mind* offers a clear and comprehensive overview of the main kinds of meditation. In "Five Ways to Know Yourself as a Spiritual Being," Shinzen Young (2007) a visionary contemporary teacher of Buddhist meditation, presents a suggestive flavor of five types within the Buddhist tradition.

In the classical Buddhist *Visudhimagga: The Path of Purification*, there are at least forty potential objects of meditation (Buddhaghosa, 1976). In this chapter, I will focus on Vipassana meditation, a core technique of classical Buddhism. Vipassana is a Pali word meaning separating things into their component parts, seeing into them, and gaining insight.

Take several moments to observe your mind. Perhaps the first thing you noticed was how difficult it was to pay attention in any sustained way. Your mind was probably filled with endless chatter: wandering thoughts, fleeting images and fantasies, transient somatic sensations. You invariably lost track of what was occurring and wandered off and were emotionally hijacked by such things as criticisms of yourself, anticipations of the future, or regrets from the past. Close inspection of your actual experience reveals that your typical mode of perception is, to an unrecognized extent, selective, distorted, and outside voluntary control. You often operate on automatic pilot, reacting to a conscious and unconscious blend of fallacious associations, anticipatory fantasies, and habitual fears that make you unaware of the actual texture of your experience. Your mind is often foggy, seldom clear, and serene. Buddhism likens the mind to a monkey endlessly jumping from branch to branch. It is difficult to see or think clearly when monkey mind prevails.

Since ordinary consciousness is usually too turbulent, preoccupied, and constricted to be attentive and focused, the mind must be trained to focus. Meditation is one deeply powerful way of doing that. Meditation is the training of moment-to-moment attentiveness—awareness without judgment of what actually happens to us instant-by-instant. Meditation involves greeting life—here and now—with focus, care, and respect. In a meditative state, we perform each task more whole-heartedly.

The *Mahasatipatthäna Sutra: The Greater Discourse on the Foundations of Mindfulness* (Translated by Maurice O'Connell Walshe, 1987) is the core Buddhist text on the meditative process. There are four "foundations to mindfulness," according to the Buddha:

1 Awareness of the body in four positions (walking, standing, sitting, and lying down).
2 Awareness of "feelings" (vedanä) —which refers to physical (or emotional) sensations of pleasantness, unpleasantness, or neutrality rather than what we call emotions.
3 Awareness of states of mind—for example, whether we are clear or distracted, angry or calm, contracted or spacious.
4 Awareness of "mind-objects"—which ranges from Buddhist notions about the hindrances to meditation (e.g. sense desire, ill-will, sloth and torpor, worry, and doubt) to the five "aggregates" or elements that make up every moment of experience (form, feeling, perception, mental-formation, and consciousness) to the Seven Factors of Enlightenment (mindfulness, investigation, energy, delight, tranquility, concentration, and equanimity) to the Four Noble Truths (the reality and pervasiveness of suffering, the cause of it, the solution, and the path to end it).

The meditative process in the Buddhist tradition consists of two steps or stages: concentration and insight. In concentrative meditation, we focus on a single object, such as the breath at the nostrils or abdomen with wholehearted attentiveness; excluding everything but the single object we are focusing on. When attentiveness is developed and stabilized, then insight meditation is practiced. In insight meditation, we nonjudgmentally note and then silently label whatever thoughts, feelings, fantasies, or somatic sensations that we experience moment-by-moment such as "planning," "judging," "regretting," and so forth.

Shinzen Young (2007) suggests that meditation cultivates two predominant traits: clarity and equanimity. Clarity regarding the components of your sensory experience—physical sensations or emotions in the body, visual thinking or internal images, and verbal thinking or internal talk—as they emerge moment-after-moment alone or in various combinations. Equanimity is an acceptance of whatever happens—the ability to meet whatever life brings—from strife to joyfulness with calm acceptance.

Meditation fosters increased attentiveness and equanimity, self-awareness and tolerance of emotions. It also lessens distractedness, quiets the inner pandemonium, reduces self-criticism, and cultivates the capacity to tolerate a greater range of emotions.

Meditation not only allows us to examine our feelings and reactions microscopically, but to watch the film that is our mind in slower motion and more clearly. "Just as the focused lens of a microscope enables us to see hidden levels of reality," notes Buddhist teacher Joseph Goldstein (2007), "so too a concentrated mind opens us to deeper levels of experience and more subtle movements of thought and emotion."

I have personally experienced this. Several times many years ago I had my own therapy sessions immediately after returning from intensive retreats that involved meditating throughout the day for two weeks. What my analyst and I both noticed was that my internal and interpersonal awareness was qualitatively heightened. I was able to detect fleeting aspects of inner experience, as well as subtle aspects of our therapeutic interaction.

I'm not alone—countless practitioners have shared my subjective experiences. Regular meditation enhances one's capacity to notice ordinarily obscure phenomena, ranging from subtle somatic sensations to subliminal feelings and ideas, creative images and insights. Meditation also lessens self-criticism and increases our tolerance of emotion. We can literally sit with and through everything from anxiety to shame, without judging these feelings, denying their existence, or attributing them to other people.

An illustration of this is my reaction to a client who had been humiliated as a child by a verbally abusive father. When she began attacking me verbally during our sessions, her contemptuous stance triggered my shame. I felt degraded and humiliated. I suspect that before I became a meditator, I would have immediately shut down or attempted to justify or defend myself. Meditation helped me lean into my embarrassment and relate to it—and her—with more compassion.

In quieting the mind and increasing our capacity to tolerate emotions, illuminating our hidden assumptions, and short-circuiting the ingrained tendency of most of us to excessively criticize ourselves, meditation deepens our attunement to other people and increases access to our capacity for empathy and creativity, intuition and wisdom. This is an extraordinary—and relatively untapped—resource for therapists, and one that serves as the foundation for genuine psychotherapeutic listening. It's the technique that Freud didn't provide us.

Listening Stereophonically

Many years ago, I was working with a difficult-to-reach latency-aged boy who had been in therapy several times but never connected with any therapist or continued treatment for very long. In an early session, one that occurred after I had done some meditation beforehand, a wisp of an image flashed into my consciousness and then immediately disappeared: a wounded bird. As we sat together in relative silence, I tried to listen stereophonically—on two channels—remaining alert to my frightened patient and attuned to my own inner experience. More came to mind about the vulnerable bird. Its wing was damaged, it couldn't fly, and it felt endangered. The slightest movement would terrify it, and its wings would flutter furiously. I began sitting back in my chair, being as still as I could, speaking more slowly and calmly so that my client would not feel terrified. Soon after, he began opening up, telling me what was frightening him.

Therapists periodically have fleeting thoughts and feelings, somatic sensations and fantasies that can aid self-understanding and the therapeutic process, but often these are so rapid and subliminal that they are missed. Meditation enhances our capacity to notice them.

In the mid-1980s, I wrote an article in which I proposed that meditation offered operationalizable techniques for cultivating precisely that special state of mind that Freud (1912) recognized was indispensable for psychoanalytic listening—namely "evenly hovering attention" (Rubin, 1985).

In the first two decades of the twenty-first century, there is great interest in how mindfulness could be used in psychotherapy. Books, articles, and conference herald the transformative properties of meditation and its potential use in treating a wide range of people and problems. This is a wonderful development; one that I am gratified has finally happened.

In an online class on meditative psychoanalysis with psychoanalytic candidates in China at The American Institute of Psychoanalysis on October 8, 2024, I proposed that we can do even better and go much further in our efforts to integrate meditation and therapy and thereby give our patients—as well as meditators—the best of both worlds.

Genuine psychotherapeutic listening—hearing the hidden and metaphoric as well as the manifest and literal meaning—requires one other quality: the capacity to decode or translate what we simultaneously hear on an *unconscious* as well as conscious level, and this is something which meditation does not do. It is a crucial weakness. I have witnessed this inability with patients who are teachers and students of meditation, as well as in my own decades-long practice of meditation.

A college student told me about a discussion she had with her Buddhist teacher in which they talked about her wish to deepen her study of Buddhism by going to a monastery in Asia for a retreat. She didn't sound very enthusiastic. And I wasn't sure why.

"Tell me more about your conversation," I said.

"I told him 'I *don't* want to go'…I mean, I want to go." She paused. "Is that a Freudian slip?" she asked, with a look suggesting she didn't need an answer.

"What comes to mind about *not* wanting to go?" I asked.

"I'm not sure," she said. "I may be pushing myself, doing it for the wrong reasons—because my boyfriend wants me to. And he may have other motives besides my well-being. Like wanting to justify what he's into. And my teacher didn't ask me if I had any hesitation—he just assumed that I wanted to go."

It is tempting to hear only the surface of what the student said to her Buddhist teacher, just as the teacher did. But then we might miss what is underneath.

"Don't get me wrong—I love Buddhism, and it's changed my life," she continued. "But it is not a panacea, and I sense certain problems with it. It can be too detached, anti-emotional, and as I've told you, I have had quite enough of that with my intellectual parents to last several lifetimes."

"I hope that Freud and his pupils will push their ideas to their utmost limits, so that we may learn what they are…" writes William James in a letter of September 28, 1909 to Théodore Flournoy, "obviously 'symbolism' is a most dangerous method" (James, 1920).

Why is it so dangerous? Because it reveals that we often say more than we *realize*. Without attention to the symbolic aspect of listening, my client's ambivalence about studying Buddhism abroad would have gone unnoticed.

Integrating Meditation and the Psychoanalytic Unconscious

Meditation provides an operationalizable technique for cultivating evenly hovering attention and thus deepening psychoanalytic listening. But one additional element is indispensable for ideal listening: understanding the language—and logic—of the unconscious, which Buddhism neglects and doesn't understand. Without an understanding of the complexity and richness of unconscious communication, one is hampered in one's understanding.

Psychoanalytic understanding of the language and logic of the unconscious complements and enriches meditative attention. While I will focus on perspectives and insights gleaned from classical and post-Freudian psychoanalysis, my remarks are applicable, with the appropriate changes, to other schools of psychotherapeutic thought.

Two aspects of the meditative method interfere with listening in this way. Meditation focuses on deconstructing experience into its component parts, rather than decoding its meaning. And meditators without exposure to psychotherapy lack an understanding of the language—and logic—of the unconscious; what lies outside awareness.

There seem to be at least three conceptions of the unconscious in Buddhism: the classical Buddhist skandhas, or subconscious aggregate of previous conditioning (Narada, 1975); the alaya-vijnana or "storehouse" consciousness of

Mahayana Buddhism—the "subjectless flow of mutually conditioning events that momentarily constitute at the surface level of consciousness something akin to an ego that experiences and reflects" (Unno, 2006); and "mushin," that state of complete un-self-consciousness and optimal responsiveness that Zen terms "no mind" (Suzuki, 1959).

But the psychoanalytic understanding of the unconscious—particularly the notion of the primary process—offers something more: namely a fertile and revolutionary conception of *unconscious communication*. This Buddhism lacks.

In the preface to the third (revised) English edition of *The Interpretation of Dreams,* Freud (1932) wrote that this book "contains the most valuable of all the discoveries it has been my good fortune to make. Insight such as this falls to one's lot but once in a lifetime" (1900, Vol. 4). One of the most revolutionary ideas was that the mind is capable of thinking in two different ways or logics. There are, to use the title of one of Freud's papers, "two principles of mental functioning," which he called the primary and secondary process. The secondary process, which Freud claimed was characteristic of conscious thought in waking life, is adapted to the realities of the external world. It is our ordinary rational and conventionally accepted way of thinking and speaking. You are using it as you think about and reflect on what you are now reading. The secondary process obeys the laws of grammar and formal logic, respects the differences between images, and acknowledges opposites and the categories (i.e. ordering principles) of space and time. My client's conscious wish to study meditation illustrates this type of thinking.

The primary process, however, is characteristic of unconscious mental activity and emerges in dreaming, artistic creations, neurotic symptom-formation, slips of the tongue (like my client made), and schizophrenic mentation. Opposites can—and often do—co-exist in primary process communications. One can, for example, love and hate the same person or wish for and fear the same thing—like my client.

The primary process is oblivious to the categories of time and space—significant facets of our psychological past are, for example, very much "alive" in the present. "The past is never dead," wrote William Faulkner (1951) in "Requiem for a Nun." "It's not even past."

The primary process is governed by processes Freud called condensation and displacement. In the former, one image in a dream or work of art or a patient's communications may stand for several different things, while in the latter, a person or image of lesser emotional significance takes precedence over someone or something of greater importance.

A client dreams, for example, that she is sitting at the end of her bed, which is on the roof of a building. She sees her dog, who is her pal, jump from the building and plunge to the ground.

As her dog plummets, she doesn't look like a dog—she resembles a blob. My client feels powerless and is devastated. We explore her associations to the images in the dream. Sitting on the edge of her bed on a roof has three meanings to her:

1   She feels that her personal life is "on edge"—in a precarious state.
2   She fears her bed will soon be "empty" if her husband takes a job abroad.
3   She is "falling" at work—losing the secure ground she used to have.

The multiple meanings concentrated within one image illustrate the process of condensation.

Displacement—the process of putting something of greater emotional meaning and intensity in a less important place—is illustrated in her associations to the dog plummeting. As she describes this horrific sight, she says that as the dog fell toward the ground, it no longer resembled itself. She sheepishly indicated that she felt that she was changing shape and feeling like a "blob"—aging and losing something vital; particularly an athleticism that was an important part of her former identity.

Even a meditatively trained mind that is highly concentrated, attentive, and focused, is greatly handicapped in deciphering the dense and fertile texture of what it is attempting to understand without comprehending the language and logic of the unconscious. In a letter/poem to Thomas Butts on November 22, 1802, William Blake writes: "And a double vision is always with me/With my inward Eye 'tis an old man Man grey/With my outward a Thistle across my way/…May God us keep/From Single vision and Newton's sleep" (quoted in Bentley, 2001). Blake was not only challenging an exclusively rationalistic view of the universe, but he was pointing toward a more inclusive kind of perception. To truly understand what Freud (1900) called the "overdetermination" of internal and interpersonal experiences—the way the "same" thought, feeling, fantasy, or action, may be motivated by various unconscious factors and have multiple unconscious meanings and functions—we need to have "double vision," to listen stereophonically, on at least two channels at once, to the manifest and the hidden meaning.

The Thirty-Seventh Zen Patriarch, Ling-yu of the Mazu lineage, lived in the ninth century. He was sitting up in bed with his eyes wide open one morning when his secretary entered the room and asked him why he had such a strange look on his face.

"I've just had a dream," the Master said. "Why don't you try to interpret it?"

The secretary bowed respectfully and left the room. Moments later, Ling-yu's assistant came in and was asked the same question. The assistant bowed and walked out.

The secretary soon returned with a tub of hot water for the Master's bath, and the assistant brought a cup of tea. Seeing that neither disciple was lured into the world of dreams, Ling-yu praised them (Taylor, 1999).

One way of interpreting this story is that the secretary and the assistant were devoted to what Zen might call life-as-it-is and were not "side-tracked" by phantoms or dreams. "Dreams, in Buddhism, can refer to deluded thoughts…

especially becoming ensnared in the trance of everyday self-absorbed think-ing...There's another view of dream in Zen, the evanescence of each moment and every phenomenon (in the Diamond Sutra): a source of delusion if we attach blindly to it, a source of play and liberation if we do not (row row row your boat)" (Bobrow, personal communication, January 15, 2007).

I suspect many centuries of Buddhists might agree.

"All things at all times teach," says the Buddhist *Avantamsaka Sutra* (Tongx-uan, 1989).

"A dream unanalyzed is like a letter unopened," it is written in the Talmud.

If everything is real—as Zen master Dogen recognizes (cf. Cook, 1978; Kim, 2004)—then dreams teach. Perhaps the secretary and the assistant, like the Master, missed an opportunity to learn when they listened on one channel instead of two.

Freud presented the primary and secondary processes as inherently anti-thetical to each other. He believed that the primary process was developmen-tally more archaic and maladaptive than the secondary process and that in healthy development it would be outgrown or mastered.

While Freud's bilingual logic of the mind is a profound contribution to human self-understanding, there are several serious defects with it—especially the fact that it is underwritten by an increasingly beleaguered mechanistic model of the mind as a mental apparatus within which imper-sonal and unruly instinctual drives circulate, press for discharge, get dammed up, and assault the besieged individual. Fewer contemporary analysts find this a compelling view of the mind, because it has been devastatingly cri-tiqued over the last several decades by Schafer (1976), Stolorow and Atwood (1979), and Greenberg and Mitchell (1983), among many others.

Freud's theory also pathologizes the primary process and makes it more primitive than the secondary process. Later analysts such as Rycroft (1956, 1962) and Loewald (1978/1980) did not believe that primary process and sec-ondary process were mutually antagonistic or that the primary process was inevitably neurotic. In fact, they viewed them as mutually enriching.

One can appreciate the profound value of the primary process as an exquisite means of unconscious communication without subscribing to—or endorsing—every aspect of Freud's immense body of work. One can, for example, challenge his mechanistic model of the mind (or his pessimistic model of health) without eliminating his stunning insights about the way we often communicate more than we know.

Aware of both the breath-taking insights and the difficulties in Freud's con-ceptualizations, both Rycroft and Loewald attempt to reformulate the primary and secondary process in such a way as to throw out the bathwater of the theoretical problems without eliminating the baby of the seminal insights.

The philosopher Suzanne Langer (1942) describes two modes of commu-nication, what she termed discursive and non-discursive symbolism—or con-scious, rational thought in words presented successively in accordance with accepted rules of grammar and logic and visual or auditory images appearing in a single instance rather than in a successive sequence. Drawing on this distinction, Rycroft unlinks the theory of the primary and secondary process from the mechanistic assumptions of Freud's defective drive model, while retaining the wisdom embedded in Freud's two principles of mental functioning. Rycroft then uses Langer to synthesize the two facets of mental functioning that Freud's theory depicts, suggesting that they are potentially cross-pollinating. In other words, we need to operate in both modes to lead a full and rich life.

Loewald (1978/1980) reconceptualizes primary and secondary processes while also disconnecting them from their original usage as modes of energetic regulation. Instead of dichotomizing these aspects of experience and privileging one over the other, he recommends integration, balance, and cross-pollination. If one lives too much in the primary process mode, then one drowns in a dysfunctional, phantasmagorical world of metaphors and images. If one resides too exclusively in a hyper-rational world of the secondary process then one lives a more emotionally shallow and impoverished life devoid of the creative and vitalizing aspects of the primary process. "We are poor indeed if we are only sane," as Winnicott (1945/1978) noted.

Optimal listening, in my view, involves two stages: (1) quieting and focusing the mind through a meditative practice and then (2) examining and investigating whatever arises with an abiding interest in the meaning of what you hear and a sensitivity to the language—and logic—of the unconscious. Attempting to listen to someone without developing heightened attentiveness is like taking a photograph with a wonderful lens held by an unsteady hand—the picture will be blurred.

Psychoanalysis falls into this trap because it lacks a method for cultivating the deep concentration and equanimity trained by Buddhist meditation.

Deep inner concentration and quietude increase our capacity for self-awareness and tolerance of feeling. When we still the normally turbulent waters of our minds, we have greater access to our emotional depths. We can literally notice more of what is occurring as well as sit through a greater range of feelings without the need to either identify with them, act on them, or push them away, as I suggested earlier.

The "meditative photographer" holds the camera completely still but uses a narrower lens and doesn't "develop" the picture. The picture will be clear, but restricted—neglecting various aspects of unconscious communication such as dreams and slips of the tongue. Listening stereophonically—on two channels at once—is a crucial aspect of a wide-angle lens.

Stereophonic listening enables us to hear symptoms—traces of old, undigested experience that constrict us in the present—and creative symbols, which are often intimations, if not harbingers, of new, inchoate, and constructive directions in one's life.

Comfort with the primary process encourages us to stay with and eventually translate or decode the meaning of unconscious communication. We literally have more access to it and greater adeptness in handling it.

For optimal psychotherapeutic listening, we need to hold the camera steady—concentrate the mind—and use a wide-angle lens. Then the picture will be both clear and more comprehensive. This is, I believe, one of the unsung gifts that the marriage of Buddha and Freud bequeaths to us.

References

Bentley, Gerard. Eades. *The Stranger from Paradise: A Biography of William Blake*. New Haven: Yale University Press, 2001. Pages 219–220.

Bion, Wilfred Ruprecht. *Attention and Interpretation: A Scientific Approach to Insight in Psycho-Analysis and Groups*. London: Tavistock Publications, 1970.

Buddha. "Mahāsatipatthāna Sutra: The Greater Discourse on the Foundations of Mindfulness." In *Thus Have I Heard: The Long Discourses of the Buddha*. Translated by Maurice O'Connell Walshe. Boston: Wisdom Publications, 1987. Pages 335–350.

Buddhaghosa, Bhadantācariya. *The Path of Purification*. Boulder: Shambhala Press, 1976. Page 99.

Coltart, Nina. "The Practice of Psychoanalysis and Buddhism." In *Slouching Toward Bethlehem*. New York: The Guilford Press, 1992. Pages 164–175.

Cook, Francis. *How to Raise an Ox: Zen Practice as Taught in Zen Master Dogen's Shobogenzo*. Los Angeles: Center Publications, 1978.

Faulkner, William. *Requiem for a Nun*. New York: Random House, 1951.

Freud, Sigmund. "The Dream Work and the Primary and Secondary Process." In The Interpretation of Dreams, Standard Edition, 4&5. London: Hogarth Press, 1900. Pages 599–609, 277–281; 305–309.

Freud, Sigmund. "Recommendations to Physicians on Practicing Psycho-Analysis." In *Standard Edition*, 12. London: Hogarth Press, 1912. Pages 111–120.

Freud, Sigmund. "Preface to the Third (Revised) English Edition of The Interpretation of Dreams." In *Standard Edition*, 4. London: Hogarth Press, 1932. Page 32.

Goldstein, Joseph. *A Heart Full of Peace*. Somerville, MA: Wisdom Publications, 2007. Page 93.

Goleman, Daniel. *The Meditative Mind: Varieties of the Meditative Experience*. Los Angeles: Jeremy Tarcher, 1988.

Greenberg, Jay R., and Mitchell, Stephen. *Object Relations in Psychoanalytic Theory*. Cambridge, MA: Harvard University Press, 1983.

James, William. *The Letters of William James*. edited by Henry James. New York: Atlantic Monthly Press, 1920. Pages 327–328.

Kim, Hee-Jin. *Eihei Dogen: Mystical Realist*. Boston: Wisdom Publications, 2004.

Langer, Susanne. "Discursive and Presentational Forms." In *Philosophy in a New Key*. Cambridge, MA: Harvard University Press, 1942. Pages 75–94.

Loewald, Hans. "Primary Process, Secondary Process, and Language." In *Papers on Psychoanalysis*. New Haven: Yale University Press, 1978/1980. Pages 178–206.

Rubin, Jeffrey B. "Meditation and Psychoanalytic Listening." *Psychoanalytic Review* 72, no. 4 1985. Pages 599–613.

Rubin, Jeffrey B. *Psychotherapy and Buddhism: Toward an Integration*. New York: Plenum Press, 1996.

Rycroft, Charles. "Beyond the Reality Principle." In *Imagination and Reality: Psycho-Analytical Essays 1951–1961*. London: Hogarth Press, 1962. Pages 102–113.

Rycroft, Charles. "Symbolism and Its Relation to the Primary and Secondary Process." In *Imagination and Reality: Psycho-Analytical Essays 1951–1961*. London: Hogarth Press, 1956. Pages 42–60.

Schafer, Roy. *A New Language for Psychoanalysis*. New Haven: Yale University Press, 1976.

Stolorow, Robert, and George Atwood. *Faces in a Cloud: Subjectivity in Personality Theory*. New York: Jason Aronson, 1979.

Suzuki, Daisetz Teitaro "Zen Swordsmanship." In *Zen and Japanese Culture*. Princeton, NJ: Princeton University Press, 1959. Pages 87–136, 110–111.

Taylor, John P. "Koans of Silence: The Teaching Not Taught." *Parabola: Myth, Tradition, and the Search for Meaning*, Spring 1999. Page 611.

Thera, Narada. *A Manual of Abhidharma; An Outline of Buddhist Philosophy*. Kandy: Buddhist Publication Society, 1975. Pages 349–351.

Tongxuan, Li. *Entry into the Realm of Reality: The Guide and Commentary on the Gandavyuha, the Final Book of the Avatamsaka Sutra*. Translated by Thomas Cleary. Boston: Shambhala, 1989.

Unno, Mark. "Introduction." In *Buddhism and Psychotherapy: Essays on Theories and Practices*, edited by Mark Unno. Boston: Wisdom Publications, 2006. Pages 7, 87–104.

Welwood, John. *Toward a Psychology of Awakening: Buddhism, Psychotherapy, and the Path of Personal and Spiritual Transformation*. Boston: Shambhala Publications, 2000. Page 75.

Winnicott, Donald W. "Hate in the Counter-Transference." In *Through Paediatrics to Psycho-Analysis*. London: Hogarth Press, 1945/1978. Page 150.

Young, Shinzen. "Five Ways to Know Yourself as a Spiritual Being." Accessed on Shinzen.org, 2007.

3 The Incomparable Power of Human Understanding

"Everything that man has handled has the fatal tendency to secrete meaning," Octavio Paz wrote in his biographical portrait, *Marcel Duchamp: Appearance Stripped Bare*. The search for understanding, one of the hallmarks of psychoanalysis, takes many forms: from detecting patterns in a person's life story to illuminating what an emotional or physical symptom or a symbol in a dream conveys. We find meaning, as Jungian analyst Ann Ulanov (2004) aptly noted, by "looking back to its cause and forward to its purpose."

Meaning can be confusing because it is sometimes disguised and can't be read on the surface. Decoding is often necessary. A person may show up late to a doctor's appointment because he is afraid of hearing bad news, the subway was delayed, or he is mad at his physician. Or none of the above.

We never know the significance of something in advance. "What is the meaning of such [flying] dreams?" asked Freud. "It is impossible to give a general reply. As we shall hear, they mean something different in every instance" (Freud, 1900).

In psychoanalysis, understanding is arrived at, as Freud (1900) recognized, not by translating what we examine into what we already know or assume, but by eliciting the client's unique associations or reactions. Otherwise, the therapist simply "discovers" his own assumptions and biases—like a scientist who thinks his accidental fingerprint on the slide belongs to the organism he is investigating.

We find meaning by paying attention to and being one with the cause and the function (or purpose) of a thought, feeling, or action, which includes the emergent potentials it embodies. For example, when a person is late to a session, hearing their own account of what happened, rather than assuming in advance what their lateness represents, is crucial. As I've shown, listening deeply on two levels or channels—conscious and unconscious—is indispensable, but unfortunately meditation training neglects the unconscious (Rubin, 2009). Buddhism describes three kinds of unconsciousness, but they are very different than—and certainly not a replacement for—psychoanalytic insights about it. Without an understanding of the complexity and richness of *unconscious communication*— a foundational discovery of psychoanalysis—one is hampered in one's understanding of other people or ourselves, as I mentioned earlier.

DOI: 10.4324/9781003598596-4

Although meditation can sometimes reveal and illuminate meaning, it can also conceal and obfuscate it. At times, the significance of an action emerges directly and automatically when we are truly one with what we are experiencing, like when you sense a child's hidden fear of disappointing you is causing them to accommodate to what they imagine you want instead of directly expressing how they feel and risking being abandoned by you. Zen Buddhism calls this *prajna* wisdom, or intuition. At other times, "being in the moment" is not enough to foster understanding; we need to step back from direct contact with a person or emotion and reflect on it—what I call *reflective intimacy*, which we'll explore in the next chapter.

One patient, a competent and compassionate thirty-nine-year-old woman, illustrated how meditation practice can inadvertently make the search for meaning more difficult. In our first session, she informed me that she was coming to therapy hoping to get a handle on her listlessness and apathy after a variety of medical tests ruled out thyroid disease, mononucleosis, and other physical ailments. Capable and popular, with friends that she valued, she felt it was increasingly difficult to engage life wholeheartedly. My patient was in a relationship that not only seemed to be going nowhere, but—she reluctantly acknowledged—was hurting her. "He is verbally abusive," she admitted. She longed to settle down before it was too late and start a family.

I learned that she was haunted by her painful childhood. She had suffered massive losses—her older sister's death from leukemia when my patient was nine, and her father's death soon after. She remembered being overwhelmed by uncontrollable outbursts of anger.

In graduate school, she discovered meditation. She practiced a Tibetan technique called "touch-and-go." She sat still and opened to whatever arose—often sorrow and loneliness—identified with these feelings momentarily, and then let them go.

In her book, *The Courage to Be Present: Buddhism, Psychotherapy, and the Awakening of* Natural Wisdom, Karen Wegela (2009), who teaches at the Buddhist institution the creator of touch-and-go, Chögyam Trungpa, founded, described the practice like this:

> When an experience arises, gently touch or taste it. Then, allow it to go, or go along…How long should you touch? I usually suggest to people that they think of how long it would take to recognize their favorite food if it were placed into their mouth while their eyes were closed. How long would it take to recognize chocolate? Or butter pecan ice cream? Or béarnaise sauce? It doesn't take too long. Touch about that long.

My client pursued meditation with passion and became highly skilled at focusing and concentrating her mind. She reported that meditating helped her cope with the intense feelings she had been prone to since her teens. "I learned," she told me very confidently, "that through meditation, I could lay my feelings about my life to rest."

Effective as it might be, her meditation also cut her off from feedback about her emotions. She didn't yet realize that addressing their meaning was vital to figuring out what haunted her. The loss and abuse that she thought were "put to rest" returned in the form of her symptoms and suffering. She had spent eighteen years anesthetizing herself with meditation, instead of dealing with the experiences of her childhood that caused her such sadness. Her apathy was a result of emotions (like grief) that begged to be felt and understood. She couldn't meditate that away. She had to experience and understand the pain to heal herself and engage her present life.

My patient called our therapy "touch-and-stay" because we contacted and stayed with her feelings of sorrow and loss in the past, and the neglect she was enduring with her boyfriend in the present. She was able to grieve and mourn. She initially felt worse, but began embracing her life more fully, and eventually passion and vitality replaced listlessness and indifference. She left her boyfriend and began dating a man who really cherished her.

When we ignore the meaning of our feelings or actions, we are condemned to repeat them. That which we disavow—for example, a Buddhist teacher's lustful feelings toward a student or his urge to anesthetize his pain through excessive drinking—festers and explodes in the form of symptoms, spiritual scandals, and self-harmful behavior. This is what Freud in his paper "Repression" (1915) called the "return of the repressed."

Meditators who engage in touch-and-stay might gain insight into at least two neglected topics in Eastern contemplative disciplines—namely, the psychological obstacles to meditation practice and the emotional ingredients of spiritual scandals. When one is resistant to meditation, one "forgets" to meditate or chronically avoids it, "does not have time to do it," or uses it to suppress or escape from pain or conflict. All of this disrupts or undermines one's practice and fosters self-blindness.

Buddhism describes various barriers to meditation—specifically, the Five Hindrances, the Ten Fetters, and the Ten Impediments (Thera, 1975; Buddhaghosa, 1976). These focus on *conscious* emotional and situational interferences to meditation, such as egoism, anger, sense desire, restlessness, blind adherence to rites and rituals, and theoretical studies divorced from practice. However, the *unconscious* psychological obstacles to meditation have not been systematically identified. Psychoanalysis, an exquisite description of unconscious strategies of self-deception and self-inhibition, can illuminate a crucial and neglected aspect of Buddhism: what interferes with developing, maintaining, and deepening meditation practice (Rubin, 1996).

Just as in the West, spiritual scandals are a recurring theme in contemporary Eastern contemplative traditions. In recent years, there have been numerous cases of Buddhist (and yoga) teachers, presumably exemplars of the highest ethical ideals, falling prey to addictive behavior, gross misuse of power, and sexual and financial scandals (e.g. Boucher, 1988; Kornfield, 1993, 2000; Rubin, 1996; Gleig & Langenberg, 2023). In "Sexual Ethics and Healthy Boundaries in the Wake of Teacher Abuse," a sobering historical study, two scholars, Ann Gleig and Amy Langenberg, demonstrated that "sexual abuse and related ethical breaches have continued across racial, generational, and lineage lines in transnational Buddhism for over four decades." This topic is either rationalized away or the participants are demonized. Rarely is the meaning and function of the lapse illuminated with compassion and insight. Why do some Buddhist teachers become embroiled in exploitative behavior? What might they do to lessen the gap between their cherished ideals and their all-too-human—or immoral—actions? What is the meaning and function of students idealizing their teachers and devaluing themselves? Why do spiritual seekers regularly substitute a teacher's wishes for their own?

Psychoanalysis can shed light on the psychology of scandals, including authoritarian teachers and submissive students, a topic we'll explore in more detail in Chapter 6, "Dancing with Desire: Shining a Psychoanalytic Light on Scandals in Buddhism."

For psychotherapists, touching and staying, and remaining with the actual experiences of our clients—and seeing them through their eyes—cultivate empathy, a key ingredient in understanding. And the same principle applies, with the appropriate changes, for patients and lay readers. In other words, when we strive to be emotionally attuned to what we encounter—from uncomfortable feelings to difficult people—we increase our capacity for understanding and responding wisely.

At the beginning of a session years ago, a young man who had been diagnosed as a paranoid schizophrenic told me he felt "dead like a mannequin." His posture was slouched, and he was devitalized for the rest of the session. Toward the end of our meeting, he suddenly had the fantasy of running out into the street and crashing into a car.

After he shared this, I strove to comprehend it from within his perspective, not mine. I asked myself what benefit he might derive from enacting what he daydreamed.

"I wonder if the actual sensation of crashing into a car would create a feeling of aliveness, and while life-threatening, if that is somehow preferable to feeling 'dead like a mannequin'?" I asked.

He bolted up in his chair and immediately became more awake and animated. During the remainder of our time together, he elaborated the reasons he felt psychologically and spiritually "dead"—he felt that we lived in a cold, materialistic world that valued profits over people.

Before I studied Zen, when I just wore my psychoanalytic hat in sessions, I would have begun my description of understanding by emphasizing a staple of contemporary therapy—namely, *empathy*, which George Atwood calls the "incomparable power of human understanding" (Stolorow, 2007). Therapists since Carl Rogers and Heinz Kohut (1959) have taught us how understanding people from within their own frame of reference, as opposed to viewing them from an outside vantage point, is an indispensable aspect of healing and transformation. While I still believe that is true, I now think that to describe the process, we have to go back a few steps and proceed more slowly.

There are at least two preconditions for being empathic: perceiving with an innocent mind, which entails holding your favorite theory—whether psychoanalytic or Buddhist—lightly as opposed to tightly and uniting and being intimate with whatever arises. Meditation is a remarkable resource for doing this.

Holding what we believe lightly is not so easy, for it not only orients us by giving us a stable identity, but it also fortifies us. Self-definition—delineating who we *are* by differentiating ourselves from who (or what) we are *not*—seems to be a quintessential human need. But it also inhibits us. We begin to listen *for* what we already believe rather than listen *to* what we are encountering. And then we only "hear" echoes of old, stale experience—*what we knew*. And we are never surprised. Like good therapy, the Buddhist notion of non-attachment—engagement without clinging—is immeasurably helpful in fostering a fresh relationship to what life presents.

In Zen Buddhism, there is a concept called *shoshin,* or beginner's mind: "In the beginner's mind there are many possibilities; in the expert's mind there are few," wrote Shunryu Suzuki (1970). We might think of this receptive outlook as *Zen-in-action*—an attitude of openness, with a lack of preconceptions. When we listen to a client or a supervisee or a spouse in this spirit, we are not the-one-who-knows. We are traveling light, with a minimum of baggage, and we are more receptive to what we encounter. Such an innocent stance helps us engage the world and each other with whole-heartedness and with newfound respect.

We relate to people more directly and intimately. We see beneath their self-protective armor and masks to their unique, priceless being; what Jack Kornfield in *The Wise Heart* calls their "inner nobility and beauty" (2008). We feel greater compassion for and connection to them.

Change and transformation entail more than listening with an innocent mind and empathic and compassionate understanding, indispensable as they are. What is also crucial is *liberating intimacy*—the new forms of human connection that the therapeutic relationship makes possible. This is the third and final facet of meditative psychoanalysis.

References

Boucher, Sandy. *Turning the Wheel: American Women Creating the New Buddhism.* New York: Harper & Row, 1988.

Buddhaghosa, Bhadantācariya. *The Path of Purification.* Boulder: Shambhala Press, 1976.

Freud, Sigmund. *The Interpretation of Dreams. Standard Edition*, 4 & 5. London: Hogarth Press, 1900. Pages 392–393.

Kohut, Heinz. "Introspection, Empathy, and Psychoanalysis." *Journal of the American Psychoanalytic Association* 7. 1959. Pages 459–483.

Kornfield, Jack. *A Path with Heart: A Guide Through the Perils and Promises of Spiritual Life.* New York: Bantam Books, 1993. Page 12.

Kornfield, Jack. *After the Ecstasy, the Laundry.* New York: Bantam Books, 2000.

Kornfield, Jack. *The Wise Heart: A Guide to the Universal Teachings of Buddhist Psychology*. New York: Bantam Books, 2008.

Rubin, Jeffrey B. *Psychotherapy and Buddhism: Toward an Integration*. New York: Plenum, 1996.

Rubin, Jeffrey B. "The Analyst's Authority." In *A Psychoanalysis for Our Time: Exploring the Blindness of the Seeing I*. New York: New York University Press, 1998. Pages 213–231.

Rubin, Jeffrey B. "Deepening Psychoanalytic Listening: The Marriage of Buddha and Freud." *American Journal of Psychoanalysis* 69. 2009. Pages 93–105.

Suzuki, Shunryu. *Zen Mind, Beginner's Mind*. Weatherhill, 1970. Page 21.

Stolorow, Robert D. *Trauma and Human Existence: Autobiographical, Psychoanalytic, and Philosophical Reflections*. London: Routledge, 2007.

Thera, Narada Maha. *Manual of Abhidhamma*. Colombo, Sri Lanka: Buddhist Publication Society, 1975.

Ulanov, Ann. *Spiritual Aspects of Clinical Work*. Einsiedeln: Daimon Verlag, 2004. Page 134.

Wegela, Karen. *The Courage to Be Present: Buddhism, Psychotherapy, and the Awakening of Natural Wisdom*. Boulder: Shambhala Publications, 2009. Page 64.

4 Liberating Intimacy

One of the seminal insights of psychoanalysis is that human development—and the psychotherapeutic relationship—always and inevitably occurs in the context of formative human relationships. "There is no such thing as an infant," psychoanalyst D.W. Winnicott (1960) famously wrote. There are only specific parent-infant dyads or triads. From my perspective, there is also no such thing as a patient, by which I mean a self-enclosed, isolated individual whose behavior is generated strictly from within; there are only specific patient-therapist relationships which shape and co-create each person's reality.

One of the hallmarks of psychoanalysis is the belief that the therapeutic relationship—the attachment or emotionally intimate connection between the analysand and the analyst—is indispensable in working through psychopathology and trauma and creating a more fulfilling life.

Psychoanalysis and Buddhism define and conceive of attachment in diametrically opposed ways. Attachment, in Buddhism, is the source of human suffering. Buddhism offers a sustained and deeply convincing critique of the dangers of craving in its myriad guises—including the clinging to our viewpoints and theories as mental health professionals, which generates psychological imprisonment, as well as vast suffering.

"Non-attachment, all I hear is non-attachment," wrote Zen scholar and teacher Katsuki Sekida (2005). "If you weren't attached, you'd be dead."

Connections with other people are, according to psychoanalysis, not only central to human growth and development; they are indispensable to survival. Without such attachments, we are doomed to alienation and stunted emotional development, immense suffering, and sabotaged relationships. What often transforms a horrible experience into a trauma is undergoing it alone, with no emotional home for one's feelings (Stolorow, 2007). Healing does not happen in isolation—it involves someone bearing witness to, and helping the traumatized person understand, their emotional agony.

Psychoanalysis, with its provision of a collaborative relationship designed to validate the client's experiences and provide opportunities for new forms of relatedness and self-transformation, enriches Buddhism. In meditative psychoanalysis, the therapeutic relationship—influenced by principles and

DOI: 10.4324/9781003598596-5

practices of Buddhist meditation—is the crucible in which we play out where we are trapped by the past. It is also the vehicle for discovering new paths to healthier living.

The therapeutic relationship, and the liberating intimacy it provides at its best, occurs in a special and unusual relationship—one characterized by empathy and profound emotional attunement, self-reflectiveness and freedom and creativity.

I have had several encounters that illuminate these qualities.

After I'd established a deep therapeutic connection and many horrific memories had surfaced for a psychoanalytic candidate with a severe trauma history, she indicated that she was feeling worse—and emotionally stuck. Lack of physical energy, dread, and mental lethargy were her constant companions. As we explored her emotions, various meanings emerged—especially the way she was terrified of being abandoned and re-traumatized by me. She seemed relieved by understanding what haunted her, but still somewhat stymied. I eventually wondered if the closeness of our relationship was increasing her misery. An important aspect of self-reflectiveness is examining the way the therapist's personality and theoretical allegiances and methods may shape—and sometimes interfere with—the treatment. Perhaps if someone she liked and respected valued her, then maybe she wasn't loathsome, which amplified the sense of betrayal by her parents who hadn't protected her from—and who denied—her trauma in the past.

As I reflected on her predicament, Kyogen's "Man Up a Tree" koan, one of those paradoxical puzzles Zen teachers give their students, came to mind. This was a question I had studied and "passed" in my own training to be a Zen teacher. A man, who is in a tree, hanging from a branch by his mouth, is asked by a man under the tree, "What is the meaning of Bodhidharma's coming from the west?" (Bodhidharma is traditionally viewed as the transmitter of Buddhism from India to China.) The man in the tree is in a desperate predicament. He will fail if he doesn't say something, and he will drop to his death if he does. We often find ourselves in a related dilemma in therapy and our lives when we must respond to something when we seemingly can't—no good options are apparent—and we don't know what to do.

The psychoanalytic candidate, like all of us, couldn't cure herself independently. She needed someone to witness and validate her trauma and pain; yet trusting—and relying on—other people was terrifying, and the act of revealing her abuse was forbidden by her abusers. They'd threatened to kill her if she did. She was an imaginative therapist and a talented artist who regularly used art (painting and collage)—and Jung's (1961, 2009) technique of active imagination, or artistically exploring symbolic imagery in dreams—to access and examine her emotions. A powerful teaching tool in Zen Buddhism are koans, paradoxical and rationally unanswerable anecdotes or riddles that students meditate on and are used to provoke a shift in perspective and an awakening. Knowing that speaking about how she was traumatized was itself traumatic, I suggested a "life koan" for her: "How can you communicate what you need to with me without talking about it?"

"I'll bring in artwork on Friday," she said with a noticeable sigh of relief.

And she did. She brought in a brightly colored mask with a closed mouth and a picture of a gun pointing toward a person. She looked terrified and lost.

"What would happen if you punctured the mask?" I asked.

She took out a pen and pierced the sealed mouth. Then she began speaking about both how she'd been traumatized by a religious cult her parents had been part of, and how she'd been forbidden to speak about it. She also revealed new aspects of her trauma and her self-silencing. "It was freeing to do that," she said. "I felt trapped and couldn't speak. Without you asking me that question, I couldn't have done it."

Since that time, she has spoken more freely and deeply about her traumas, is more engaged in treatment, and has even begun her own integrative practice of psychotherapy, skillfully blending psychoanalysis, art, and meditation.

Practicing psychoanalysis may not be an "'impossible' profession," as Freud (1937) infamously suggested, but it surely is a complex and difficult one. Understanding another person takes unusual patience and focus, humility and experience. A crucial way mental health professionals attempt to ground themselves and lessen maddening uncertainty is by placing patients into pre-set diagnostic categories and boxes. These maps are reassuring. They are also illusions, for they put infinitely complex individuals into rigid and static pigeonholes. When the map becomes more important than the people we try to help, their individuality and the specificity of their suffering gets lost. Good therapy comes from an opposite direction. In meditative psychoanalysis, the therapist is a *"jazz improviser"* who is grounded in the fundamentals of human development and the therapeutic relationship and who can respond creatively and effectively in the moment based on the needs and demands of the particular patient; rather than a "customs official" who knows in advance what is "foreign" or "illegal" and is vigilant that nothing dangerous is smuggled in (Rubin, 1998; 2025).

Let me illustrate this with a story about a client I saw many years ago. They sat together on my couch: a brilliant and cantankerous thirteen-year-old boy, and his mother, an accountant. Actually, she sat, and he fidgeted and sank down, at one point putting his head on her lap. She was at her wits' end: her husband had killed himself the year before, and her son was desolate and depressed to the point of being suicidal. She did most of the talking and related the horrific details of the tragedy she and her son had endured in the past year. They had both lost the person most important to them, a man with a commanding personality and titanic intellect, who alternately challenged and fiercely loved his son. The boy said little. He was busy checking me out and gauging whether I could be trusted. He had spent the previous year seeing a variety of psychiatrists and psychologists, none of whom had connected with him.

As I ended the session, I got up from my chair and stood near the door. My prospective patient lumbered toward me, his mother at his flank.

"All psychiatrists are assholes," he informed me.

"There are two problems with your statement," I said. "One, I am a psychoanalyst, not a psychiatrist. Two, given your supposed intelligence—why did it take you so long to figure out my limitations?"

"I'm going to poison my mother," the boy replied.

"Thank you," I said.

"You can't say thank you, you're a shrink," he responded, momentarily flustered, trying for damage control.

"Well, you've given me a new strategy I can employ against stubborn teenage boys," I told him.

The tiny half-smile on the right side of his mouth showed me I'd hit home.

I didn't consciously plan my response. When my teenage patient challenged me at the door, my mind was free of preconceptions, receptive to his tone of voice and the vulnerability underneath his apparent hostility.

It can be scary to be without a map or a compass, a particular theory or set response to draw on. My experience over the years has cultivated a deep faith in the capacity of patients to creatively communicate what they feel and need but cannot always say. My ability to hear was infinitely increased when I put aside both what I thought I knew and any rigid and inflexible ideas about how therapy should proceed. And that provided access to a state of mind I mentioned earlier that Japanese artists, meditators, and martial artists call *mushin*, or *no-mindedness*, what D.T. Suzuki (1971) described as awareness-without-self-consciousness. No-mindedness, a state of great receptivity and flexibility, fosters the therapist's own freedom and creativity, central ingredients in the patient's transformation.

Here is what this looks like in practice. Years ago, I treated a ten-year-old boy from a single-parent home with a devoted, but nervous mother. She sent him to me because he was isolated, didn't have many friends, and appeared to be hidden. Several months later, after therapy had been going well and he had spoken about deeper concerns, he began a session in a way I have never encountered before or since. When I opened the door to my office, he rushed in and sat in the chair I always occupied. I sat in his chair. He picked up my phone as if he were calling someone. I cupped my hand around my mouth as if I were telling him a secret and whispered the following question: "What is happening?"

"I...I mean *he*, is making a phone call," he replied.

"Who is he calling?" I asked.

"The boy's parents," he said.

"I thought I could trust Jeff," I said.

I paused.

"Keep going," he said with a triumphant giggle.

"I hope Jeff is not calling my mother and telling her private things I told him," I said. "Then I could never trust him again and wouldn't open up anymore."

"Okay, we can stop," he said, as he got up from my chair and went to the seat he usually occupied.

I got up and sat in the chair he had vacated.

Soon after, new material emerged about how upset he was that his younger sister was born, making him feel abandoned and neglected.

These three cases have hopefully given you a flavor of the essential ingredients characterizing the therapeutic relationship in meditative psychoanalysis—empathy and emotional attunement, self-reflectiveness and freedom and creativity—which facilitates liberating intimacy, which refers to new kinds of human connections made possible in and by therapy.

References

Freud, Sigmund. *Analysis Terminable and Interminable. The Standard Edition of the Complete Psychological Works of Sigmund Freud, Standard Edition*, 23. London: Hogarth Press, 1937. Pages 209–253, 248.

Jung, Carl G. *Memories, Dreams, Reflections*. New York: Random House, 1961.

Jung, Carl G. *The Red Book*. Translated by Sonu Shamdasani. New York: W. W. Norton, 2009.

Rubin, Jeffrey B. "The Analyst's Authority." In *A Psychoanalysis for Our Time: Exploring the Blindness of the Seeing I*. New York: New York University Press, 1998. Pages 31–56, 180.

Rubin, Jeffrey B. *Psychotherapy Case Studies: Escaping the Prison You Didn't Know You Were In*. New York: Routledge, 2025.

Sekida, Katsuki. *The Gateless Gate*. Boston: Shambhala Publications, 2005. Pages 38–41.

Stolorow, Robert D. *Trauma and Human Existence: Autobiographical, Psychoanalytic, and Philosophical Reflections*. New York: Routledge, 2007.

Suzuki, Daisetz Teitaro. *Zen and Japanese Culture*. Princeton: Princeton University Press, 1971.

Winnicott, Donald Woods. "The Theory of the Parent-Infant Relationship." In *The Maturational Processes and the Facilitating Environment*. New York: International Universities Press, 1960. Pages 37–55.

Part II
Examples of Meditative Psychoanalysis

5 Psychoanalysis and Zen

Partners in Healing

Sam, a middle-aged man, consulted with me because he felt profoundly alienated and utterly alone. He was, from all accounts, an immensely talented and maverick Zen teacher who was, however, riddled with intense anxiety and assaulted by dread.

In our first sessions, I was immediately struck by how present he was. He listened deeply. Nothing seemed to escape his attentive ears and watchful eyes. He was unusually open and disarmingly honest; down-to-earth, without pretense or guile. He displayed a non-defensiveness that, many years later, still deeply impresses me.

I also admired his self-awareness and his capacity for self-reflection. He had an unusual capacity for exploring what he was experiencing, staying directly with a wide range of emotions, and tracking patterns in relationships. I attributed this to his deep meditative practice—and his capacity for direct experience—more than to his formidable intellect.

In the early sessions, I learned that he came by his pessimism, melancholy, and loneliness honestly. Both of his parents were alcoholics. His father had little contact with him; he showed up drunk occasionally, was completely uninvolved, and offered no emotional or concrete assistance. "I hate my father beyond belief," he said.

He learned from his grandparents that his mother had used his skin as an ashtray and had beaten him with a brine-dipped switch. She left when he was three.

He was raised by his grandparents, who "hated each other, and hardly ever spoke." The resounding abandonments and emotional neglect were "devastating." He became ashamed and intolerant of his own needs. This led to massive self-deprivation. He assumed he "must have somehow been worthless to the core." But he couldn't figure out what he had done wrong. The fantasy of essential badness and inadequacy shadowed him and never was touched or transformed by decades of intensive Zen practice, leaving him feeling bereft and angry.

A gifted student who drew great solace from language and ideas, he devoted his considerable talents to scholastic pursuits and athletics. He graduated first

DOI: 10.4324/9781003598596-7

in his high school class at sixteen and at twenty from college with high honors. He was accepted into a doctoral program abroad in literature.

During that same period in his life, a friend exposed him to Zen. He took to it immediately. He read no Zen literature—not wanting to intellectualize or contaminate the process—and just meditated. At his first Zen retreat, the teacher said, "Kill the watcher." Sam found this easy and natural.

He gave up his recently acquired tenured professorship and became a full-time student of Zen.

At his first retreat, he reached *kensho*—he had an enlightenment experience where he felt one with everything. The boundaries between inner and outer evaporated, and he saw through and to the depths of his constructed sense of self. "I felt as if something like an earthquake or an implosion was about to happen," he wrote in an unpublished autobiography.

> Everything around me looked exceedingly odd, as if the glue separating things had started to melt… By the time I got to my room I was weightless; there was no gravity. Then the earthquake or implosion—body and mind dropping off—occurred. There was an incredible explosion of light coming from inside and outside simultaneously, and everything disappeared into that light…there was no longer a here versus there, a this versus that…I understood nothing except that nothing would ever seem the same to me…And despite the fact that I had no understanding whatever of what had happened (nor do I now), this experience changed my life completely.

Sam's meditative practice and his insights continued to expand and ripen during his studies with Zen masters from several different lineages.

However, his relationships with several of them also increased his alienation. More than once, he left when he was slated to succeed—undermining his place and visibility in the Zen world—because his teachers became embroiled in sexual or financial scandals. Whereas most of the students turned a blind eye to the way these supposedly enlightened spiritual leaders sexually exploited female students or shamelessly used members of the community to build a spiritual empire, he refused to compromise his principles in order to keep his standing with them. He exposed—and left—each teacher.

When his wife betrayed him—he found her in bed one day with another man—it merely confirmed his deep-seated belief that he was worthless and there was no place on earth for him. In psychotherapy, he realized that he had never really been emotionally seen by his wife.

Themes of abandonment and neglect, passivity and invisibility took center stage in our work. We got clearer about how his parents, his doctoral advisor, and some Zen teachers had abandoned him, and how he currently neglected himself, personally and professionally.

Several months after talking about abandonment and neglect, he didn't show up for three weeks, citing sickness and snowstorms. Instead, he called me, and we held phone sessions. At the beginning of the third phone session, he said, "Please don't abandon me."

The irony hit me like a gale force wind. "I'm staring at my empty couch," I said, gently but firmly. *"You* are the one doing the abandoning...Are you abandoning yourself the way you have always been abandoned?"

"I never thought about it that way," he said. "I think there is something profoundly disturbing and true about that."

In the weeks ahead, he went through a phase of fear and depression—he was afraid that he'd never get beyond self-neglect and dejected as he awakened to what he had done to himself. "I got frightened that for ages I had abandoned my life," he said. "I realized that my response to being abandoned was to abandon myself and neglect myself. In therapy, I'm learning that the shadow side of Buddhism is the notion of no-self, which can lead to self-abandonment and self-neglect." He believed that this aspect of psychotherapy was consistent with Zen master Bodhidharma's interpretation of the precept of not killing as "not nursing a view of extinction"—not trying to eliminate aspects of our humanness.

It was not long after this revelation that Sam began to appear more buoyant and less melancholic. He was more visible, less isolated, and more engaged. He was eager to make his life his own.

Toward the end of treatment, the Zen master said: "It is a source of great pathos to reflect that without psychotherapy I might have died without having been reunited with myself! And in that sense, without having truly lived."

"I don't feel divided anymore," he added, "and I finally know what I want: to be at ease within my own skin." He felt joy, he said—the joy, I suspect, of a man who was on the road to living a life that he could honestly call his own.

Listening stereophonically—on two levels at once—aided me in understanding the core emotional dilemmas that afflicted Sam. This sympathetic understanding generated an atmosphere of safety and trust. And relating to him freshly and flexibly opened up new vistas in his life.

Psychoanalysis and Buddhism pursued in tandem often yield surprising results. The former aids the latter in handling a challenging problem: scandals in Buddhism.

6 Dancing with Desire

Shining a Psychoanalytic Light on Scandals in Buddhism

The spaciousness which meditation practice offers psychoanalysis is a wonderful gift, yet it is not a panacea, as the scandals in Buddhist centers—communities of potential capaciousness—unfortunately remind us. In recent years Buddhist communities in the Zen, Vipassana, and Tibetan traditions have been rocked by recurrent sexual and substance abuse and financial scandals. From Sogyal Rinpoche, the prominent Tibetan Buddhist lama, who established the international Rigpa community and wrote the bestselling *Tibetan Book of Living and Dying*, to Lama Norlha Rinpoche, founder of New York's Thubten Chöling Monastery, there have been numerous incidents of teacher misconduct involving Buddhist teachers from Asia as well as the United States—supposedly self-realized beings who are paragons of self-awareness and health, wisdom and compassion—sexually exploiting non-consenting students, illegally expropriating funds from their communities, and struggling with substance abuse (e.g. Boucher, 1988; Kornfield, 1985, 1993, 2000; Rubin, 1996; Magid, 2008; Deveaux, 2017; Remski, 2020; Gleig & Langenberg, 2023). Matthew Remski, who draws on investigative research and real survivors stories to elucidate cults and authoritarian extremism in Buddhism and yoga, interviewed "close to fifty ex-Shambhala [a prominent, world-wide Tibetan Buddhist community] members," who reported "every type of mistreatment imaginable, from emotional manipulation and extreme neglect to molestation and rape."

Recent practical efforts to bring about justice and build in guidelines and protections are a salutary development. In the Sangha Sutra, a fifty-one page booklet documenting the history of abuse at Zen Center of Los Angeles, Egyoku Nakao Roshi, the Senior Dharma teacher at ZCLA, offered recommendations for reform. In "Breaking the Silence on Sexual Misconduct," Lama Willa Baker (2018), a Tibetan Buddhist teacher and survivor of sexual abuse by her Buddhist teacher, offers four constructive suggestions: (1) education about power dynamics and healthy boundaries; (2) "a teacher's code of ethics, a formal grievance procedure, and training in liability for the board of directors"; (3) hearing the voices of women and men who have been exploited; and (4) holding Buddhist teachers who are embroiled in scandals accountable.

DOI: 10.4324/9781003598596-8

But too often the scandals have been denied, ignored, or rationalized away by Buddhist teachers, community leaders and board members, as scholars Ann Gleig and Amy Langenberg (2023) have detailed. One strategy of evasion is to treat any examination of the scandals as a violation of Buddhist ethics and a sign of disrespect and heresy. Not speaking ill of another person, a valuable part of Buddhist ethics, is used to censor critical reflection—and serves to insulate Buddhist teachers from scrutiny—even if the teacher has been involved in harmful behavior to other people. Orgyen Tobgyal Rinpoche, a Tibetan lama, for example, decried the eight long-term students of Sogyal Rinpoche, who wrote to the latter and confronted him about his abusive and unethical behavior. Unquestioned devotion to Buddhist teachings or teachers, from this perspective, demands silence, which unfortunately can also lead to denial and secrecy. It's unclear, however, where one draws the line between following useful ethical guidelines and a self-serving rhetoric of avoidance that tacitly whitewashes, condones, and perpetuates suffering.

While there is, of course, a danger that examining the scandals can lead to excessive recrimination and blame; avoidance, as opposed to honest and compassionate engagement, is, I suspect, hardly a quintessentially Buddhist virtue. In fact, it could be argued that the spirit of Buddhism is best honored by engaging the scandals and the reactions and exploring how they could be used as a vehicle for awakening.

"I teach one thing and one thing only. Suffering and the end of suffering," the Buddha is reputed to have said. One then wonders if it's a violation of the spirit of Buddhism for teachers or students to turn a blind eye toward actions—like those involved in the scandals—that caused suffering.

Buddhist editor and author Rick Fields wrote an article describing the essence of the crisis in his Buddhist community involving Osel Tendzin, a dharma heir of Trungpa Rinpouche, one of the leading figures in Tibetan Buddhism in American, who knowingly infected unsuspecting students with the AIDS virus. The article was censored by prominent members of the community, went unpublished, and Osel Tendzin fired Fields. When the board of directors did not support Fields he resigned, saying that Buddhist teachings in the West "would be best served in the long run by openness and honesty, painful as it may be" (quoted in Butler, 1990).

The Dalai Lama would concur. In a meeting with Western Buddhist teachers in 1993 he urged them not to be afraid of criticizing corrupt gurus: "If you cannot find any other way of dealing with the problem," he said, "tell the newspapers."

Another way of attempting to minimize and squelch the scandals is to claim that they are simply misunderstandings due to cultural differences arising when Asian teachers from traditional societies and more hierarchical institutions encounter the individualistic and hedonistic West, with students who are more open about sexuality and less deferential toward authority. But this subtly denigrates Buddhist teachers; suggesting they don't have enough self-awareness, self-control, and ethical grounding to follow their Buddhist ethics and resist these cultural influences.

Claiming that the scandals are caused by too much power invested in one person (the teacher) leading to excessive temptation; or that scandalous behavior is the "crazy-wisdom" of visionary, enlightened Buddhists that the uninitiated can't understand are two other means of suppressing inquiry.

John Welwood's (2000) otherwise highly illuminating examination of genuine and counterfeit spiritual authority illustrates another form denial takes. While skillfully elucidating the psychology of counterfeit spiritual teachers and the cults they lead, his study never mentions Buddhism in general or his own scandal-ridden Buddhist community in particular. And yet, two teachers involved in the scandals—a married teacher who slept with numerous female students, abused alcohol, and died in his late forties of liver damage (Trungpa Rinpoche) and the Dharma heir he appointed who knowingly infected unsuspecting students with AIDS (Osel Tendzin)—were leading figures in the school of Tibetan Buddhism that informs his work.

The Koan of Buddhist Scandals

Even when the scandals are confronted—as they were in a meeting between the Dalai Lama and twenty-two Western Buddhist teachers in Dharamsala in 1993 to discuss "teacher ethics, alcohol abuse and sex in the forbidden zone" and other topics relevant to the transmission of Buddhism to the West—more light was shone on practical responses to sexually abusive teachers than on the underlying psychological dynamics and causes. The behavior of the teachers who abused sex was linked to pride and intoxicants—and to students who failed to examine sufficiently the teacher's ethical and spiritual qualities—and the students and teachers who found out about it were encouraged to speak out (Batchelor, 1994).

Recent efforts to address these scandals and establish codes of conduct and educational programs, legal constraints and emotional validation and support like Lama Willa Baker recommended, offer the promise of constructive reforms. But as I reflect upon these salutary efforts I wonder as a psychoanalyst who has treated abusers and survivors if something vital is missing. The reasons for and the meanings of the scandals and the tools for addressing abuses of power and sex, money and intoxicants among Buddhist teachers seem conspicuously absent—leaving us with disquieting questions: Why are Buddhist teachers involved in such un-Buddhist behavior? How do we lessen the chances of further scandals?

The absence of psychological understanding about the scandals creates a situation in which they are bound to erupt and further undermine Buddhist communities.

From a psychoanalytic perspective, the scandals are inevitable rather than surprising. They are foreseeable for two reasons—the unruly and destabilizing nature of unconsciousness and the complexity of relationality—the nature and dynamics of what happens when two people come together to pursue an intimate relationship, engage in psychoanalytic treatment, or teach and study Zen. Here psychoanalysis has a potentially huge contribution to make to Buddhism.

Many assume that Buddhist teachers are beyond self-blindness. For those spiritual seekers who are experiencing what psychoanalyst Heinz Kohut (1971) called an "idealizing transference" to their teacher, by which I mean, a longing to merge with or lean on someone who is viewed as all-knowing, strong, and wise, such a possibility is enormously reassuring.

"The unconscious is another word for the death of the guru," writes Adam Phillips (1996), which I take to mean, you can't assume that anyone— whether a Buddhist teacher or an analyst—is either devoid of self-blindness or infallible. The claim that a Buddhist teacher is without unconsciousness is about as likely as an analyst never experiencing countertransference or blind spots again. That Buddhism has pockets of unconsciousness is suggested by three things: the residues of pathology found in enlightened meditators (e.g. Brown & Engler, 1980, 1986); the rash of scandals in Buddhist communities and the nature of consciousness (Rubin, 1996).

Rorschach studies of advanced meditation practitioners (Brown & Engler, 1986) suggested that they had intrapsychic conflict; struggles with dependency; needs for nurturance; and fear of destructiveness (Brown & Engler, 1986). Buddhist claims about the possibility of living without self-deception or self-blindness seem much more dubious once you understand the nature and pervasiveness of unconsciousness.

Psychoanalysis is a "hermeneutics of suspicion" (Ricoeur, 1970), by which I mean, it questions and often demystifies conventional and unquestioned assumptions about motives and meanings.

Psychoanalysis can help Buddhists detect where they neglect unconsciousness and are being self-deceptive—where, for example, a Buddhist teacher's expectation of unquestioning loyalty from his students hides a fragile sense of self or a wish for domination and exploitation and self-abasement in a student of Buddhism can masquerade as loyalty.

Psychoanalysis teaches Buddhism that much psychological conditioning and emotional strife cannot be transcended or eliminated. This may be less true of Zen, in which there seems to be greater emphasis on *experiencing* rather than *transcending* experience. If one cannot let go of aversive experience such as physical pain in Zen practice then one is encouraged to be the pain. Many meditators have experienced the way pain shifts or evaporates when one does this. But this strategy may not work as well with certain experiences that our patients struggle with such as intense self-criticism, interpersonal challenges, or severe trauma. The Dalai Lama was shocked to hear that Americans suffered from "self-directed contempt" (Goleman, 1997). He told a group of American scientists and mental health professionals that this experience was absent from Tibetan culture.

Psychoanalysis can enlighten Buddhists about where unconsciousness and transference and countertransference live in its theories, institutions, and practices.

Zen and Tibetan Buddhism occur in the context of an emotionally intense relationship between a teacher and student (at least for the student). The teacher might relate to the student in such a way as to challenge the student's internalized and limiting beliefs about herself and others—examples of which abound in the Zen and Tibetan literature—see, for example, the koan entitled "Bodhidharma's Mind-Pacifying" in which Bodhidharma's successor (Huike) complained to Bodhidharma of a troubled mind and asked him to grant him peace. "Show me your mind!" Bodhidharma replied. "I can't find my mind" the successor said. "I've granted you peace," replied Bodhidharma (Sekida, 1995). But neither the student nor the teacher reflect upon interpersonal dynamics or the patient's characteristic ways of relating to (and sometimes inhibiting and sabotaging) intimacy with self and other. Those are not categories endemic to (Zen or Tibetan) Buddhism. The absence of a map designed to investigate and illuminate the patient's recurrent ways of relating to self and others makes it impossible to understand and transform the patient's typical patterns of and blockages to interpersonal relationships and intimacy.

The hallmark of psychoanalysis in the last several decades is the "relational revolution," the recognition across various schools of analytic thought, that relationships with other people—real and fantasized, in the world and internalized—are both the foundation of human development and the crucible of change in therapy in the present. The relational revolution has two major lessons to teach Buddhists about the teacher-student relationship: It delineates some of the typical obstacles to genuine emotional intimacy that may arise between them and it offers a unique approach to emotional life and intimacy.

A Thief of Preconception

One Zen student's account of his relationship with his Zen teacher illustrates the first way psychoanalysis could enlighten Buddhists about the teacher-student relationship.

Larry was bright and talented, but plagued by massive self-doubt and self-consciousness. The son of an insecure, needy, and critical father, who had a passion for self-denigration and a hearty dose of jealousy for his son's intermittent joy, it was not surprising that Larry, now a grown man and a professional writer and passionate student of Zen, was brooding and obsessive. Among other things, Larry's relationship with his father sowed the seeds of self-doubt and the wish to please.

A short and portly man with a sharp mind, large and elusive brown eyes that seem brooding and mournful, and a restless, fickle manner, his Zen teacher, Tetsugen, believed that the "foundation of Zen" is intimacy—"the actualization of nonseparation" (Tworkov, 1994) between self and other.

Zen, for Tetsugen, was about centered movement, not tranquility pur-
chased by playing it safe and avoiding risk. Tetsugen relished challenging
his students and making them "uncomfortable" (Tworkov, 1994). "That's my
job," he said, "to take the net away" (Tworkov, 1994). "More than once he
indicated that keeping the community on the financial edge helped create the
very unpredictability most suitable for Zen training" (Tworkov, 1994).

A man of action whose dharma name "Tetsugen" meant "'to penetrate' the
stuff that's right in front of you" (Tworkov, 1994), he displayed little interest in
the "origins of behavioral patterns or in psychological descriptions": "If you
want to find out why you behave in a particular way, go to a therapist. If you
want to find out how to let go, practice [meditation]…I'm not so interested in
the question why? I'm more interested in how" (Tworkov, 1994).

Ambitious and self-serving, melancholic and detached, Tetsugen was a
highly skilled organizer with insatiable ambitions for expanding his Zen
community—called by some the "Zen Hilton" (Tworkov, 1994)—into various
commercial and social action projects. His optimistic financial projections
were characteristically unrealistic, leaving the community habitually overex-
tended and creating frequent cash-flow crises. "An organization without a cash
flow problem," he liked to say, "is one that isn't growing" (Shainberg, 1995).

Because his business and social action-oriented Zen was very different
from traditional Japanese teachings or monasteries focused on hard work and
work practice; or the Zen that the students had been exposed to by popular
writers such as D. T. Suzuki; it required an implicit trust in the teacher.

Trying to build an empire had its cost. Being perpetually on the financial
brink undermined the Zen community, depleting its membership and eroding
trust in its leadership and mission. Tetsugen was criticized by the board of
directors for wearing two hats. Many students left because of the emphasis on
business, rather than sitting meditation.

Once, when the community couldn't pay its mortgages, Larry became
solicitous and overprotective. In the midst of intensive practice, Tetsugen
asked him to ask his father for a loan.

Larry felt betrayed and angry.

Tetsugen asked Larry to be part of a special flagship program. Larry agreed.
When Larry was scheduled to present a Zen text Tetsugen didn't show up. "A
'personal crisis' is rumored—a romantic entanglement with a female student"
(Shainberg, 1995). The program, like many others Tetsugen started, fell apart
and was canceled, a casualty of what he liked to call his "management by
meandering" (Shainberg, 1995). Tetsugen took a one month sabbatical. He
ran into Larry at breakfast a few days after his return. He spoke of wanting to
build "townhouses" for members of the community, a $100,000 loan he was
negotiating and his plans to make it a gift in a few months. Would Larry mind
advancing the community $500 for monk robes that won't be ordered for two
years, Tetsugen asks?

Larry knows that "the community is in urgent need to pay its staff"
(Shainberg, 1995). Tetsugen tells Larry of an upcoming meeting in which

he'll propose a venture that will solve the community's financial problems. The staff at the Zen center—already overtaxed and unable to keep the zendo clean—will handle cooking, cleaning, and maintenance for a nearby yacht club that lost its manager and chef. When Larry balks, raising reasonable objections—aren't we already overstaffed, will the staff want to be busboys and wait tables, won't all this commerce distract from meditation practice?—the teacher mocks Larry's uptight ego, middle-class background, and wealthy parents who spoiled him. What could be better for you, Tetsugen reasons, than waiting on tables of rich people who treat you with contempt?

Disenchanted with Tetsugen, Larry left the Zen center and felt relieved to be free of the "looming, oppressive authority figure" (Shainberg, 1995) that had been with him for so long.

Larry's acquiescence and accommodation was quite familiar, being the way he characteristically related to his father. He transferred onto his teacher the power and authority he attributed to his father and the need to be valued he did not receive from him. Psychoanalysis calls this repetitive dance of misapprehension and misunderstanding—in which the unrequited yearnings and expectations from the past are evoked in the present—transference.

This was the experience of Natalie Goldberg who writes, "Unknowingly, [Katagiri] Roshi [her Zen teacher] became my mother, my father, my Zen master" in *The Great Failure: My Unexpected Path to Truth* (2004). Relating to someone in the present like we did to significant figures in our past is a ubiquitous phenomena according to psychoanalysis.

And yet, despite its pervasiveness, transference is, as Buddhist teacher Jack Kornfield (1993) notes, "rarely addressed in spiritual communities." Psychoanalysis has deeply enriched our understanding about many kinds of transferences, including typical ones that haunt spiritual communities.

Idealization and self-submission is a frequent dynamic in spiritual communities. When the student puts the teacher on a pedestal, the student is almost inevitably in a diminished position. "I made him [Katagiri Roshi] perfect," admits Goldberg (2004). "I was driven to get what I had longed for in my family." She eventually realizes after his death, "I could have come closer to his humanity—and mine. But I wasn't ready or willing. I had a need for him only to be great, to hold my projections. In freezing him on a pedestal I had only contributed to his isolation."

The tortured justifications of students of Buddhism who rationalize away the behavior of Buddhist teachers who abuse power and sex, money and intoxicants grows on this soil and resembles the psychological dynamic in abusive families, in which the child takes the abuser off the hook and blames herself in order to maintain an emotional connectedness with the abusive parent(s) and keep alive the possibility of receiving the love that has not been forthcoming. It is not surprising that many students accorded Osel Tendzin unquestioned loyalty.

And students did the same with Richard Baker Roshi, Suzuki Roshi's dharma heir, who was asked to leave the San Francisco Zen Center after it was discovered that he had expropriated money from the community as well as slept with various students including the wife of his best friend (Tworkov, 1994).

Idealization is a natural developmental process that is necessary for the child's growth and development; shaping the formation of guiding values and providing direction and inspiration.

But it is Janus-faced: it can also enslave and undermine.

A child like Larry, who lacked exposure growing up to viable idealizable figures or role models, becomes what psychoanalysts Heinz Kohut and Ernest Wolf (1978) calls an "ideal-hungry personality" who searches for other people to admire for their stature and power, intelligence or beauty. The idealized connections Larry sought to feel worthwhile jibed all too well with Tetsugen's need to carry out his spiritually expansionist agenda; perhaps causing him to respond to Larry's dependency needs—and perhaps his own emptiness—by using Larry for his own wishes and ends.

Countertransference, the analyst's counter-reaction to the patient's transference, is a crucial facet of the psychoanalytic process. It is no longer viewed, as it was by Freud (1910), as simply an obstacle or interference, as I mentioned in Chapter 1. It is now treated as an indispensable source of knowledge and understanding; a key element in change; a way of potentially accessing hidden aspects of the patient's dissociated present and past.

"The idea is not to get hooked," a Buddhist teacher tells a patient of mine. Getting hooked certainly can be problematic. Buddhism does a wonderful and revolutionary job of illuminating the way that "attachment"—a grasping and clinging state of mind in which we attempt to hold on to and possess inevitably transient experiences—leads to constricted space, and suffering.

But the relational perspective in psychoanalysis teaches us that getting snagged and finding a new way through may often be central to cure and transformation in the therapeutic relationship. From a relational perspective, the Buddhist teacher, like the therapist, is not an objective, masterful observer who detects transference and monitors countertransference, but a non-neutral and subjective participant who inevitably enacts and repeats important dramas from his and the patient's past. Enactments—doing what one is (and sometimes what one is not) talking about—are inevitable, ubiquitous, and potentially useful; they often offer an opportunity to play out one's transferences (and countertransferences), and connect to one's buried history, and thereby deepen and enrich the therapeutic work.

What if Tetsugen had felt the seductive pull of Larry's making him into an authority figure and then tried to help Larry discover new and more self-affirming ways of connecting and relating to other people instead of repeating with Tetsugen the problematic "terms of endearment" Larry had experienced with his parents in the past?

Zen teacher and psychoanalyst Barry Magid's (2002) discussion of a fatal conflict and impasse between a Buddhist teacher and his student illustrates one way to detect countertransferential enactments:

> A student came to me to discuss an impasse that had arisen with his [Buddhist] teacher. Although he had studied with this teacher for over a decade, both he and the teacher had concluded that he could no longer be that teacher's student. The student explained to me that in recent years (he was now in his forties) his back had started giving him trouble. He found it increasingly difficult to do the full bows that were part of the Buddhist service and that were also done for extended periods of 'bowing practice.' After his last sesshin, he had been laid up for several days with back spasms. He therefore asked his teacher to be excused from this practice, fully expecting him to understand his problem. However, the teacher told him to do the bows. Everyone has one kind of difficulty or another, his teacher said, including physical pain. If his back hurt, that was simply something he had to practice with.

Aware of the way his experiences with his distant and perfectionistic father might shape his reaction to his teacher, the student tried to talk to the teacher about the old feelings and memories that had been stirred up by the teacher's response to him. But the teacher pushed that aside, indicating that that was the past; Zen focused on the present. The teacher treated the student the way his father did, who never took the time to understand him; shattering the teacher's relationship with the student. To remain with his teacher felt like masochistic compliance for the student and such submission appeared to be what the teacher demanded to continue their relationship (Magid, 2002).

For a relationally oriented analyst, enactments, like countertransference, are often revelatory. This student's meditation practice might have been deepened if his teacher had wondered about his impact on the student—the way that he was being like the student's father by insisting that the student conform to a one-size-fits-all model of spiritual practice. Not only might a long and productive relationship not have been sabotaged and sacrificed, but the contrast between his critical and invalidating father and the self-reflective Zen teacher might have aided the student in recognizing—and no longer internalizing—his automatic tendency to blame himself for his father's attitude and behavior and accommodate to the wishes of his father, as well as father-surrogates. The malignant past often more readily emerges as problematic in the light of a more benign present (Ferenczi, 1933). If the present is like the past then the latter just seems to be the ways things are. The student's challenging of his teacher might have been incredibly transformative; representing the first faint pulsings of authenticity on his part (Rubin, 1998).

But the Buddhist relationship to emotion makes it nearly impossible for a Buddhist teacher to have the kind of relation to feelings that the relational revolution encourages. Let's say that a Buddhist teacher feels faint guilt about an erotic liaison with a student in which the student obviously got hurt and suffered. The guilt is inchoate, tenuously held. Since it makes the teacher feel badly about himself, he quickly banishes it from his consciousness. He believes—and Buddhism gives him no reason to challenge this delusion—that "letting go" of his "attachment" to guilt in the present—or treating it as "empty"; devoid of inherent, self-sufficient existence, means he's free of it. But consciously disavowing identification with something does not mean that one is not defined by it, as psychopaths who are not attached to the feelings of other people or the impact of their behavior—yet still act in destructive ways—painfully illustrate.

But guilt can be feedback that there's a gap between a Buddhist teacher's consciously held ideals of selflessness and compassion and his egocentric and immoral behavior. Exploring both this terrain as well as what he can learn about himself and his student's habitual ways of relating—was the student, for example, merely a passive and vulnerable victim of his entreaties or did she have any complicity?—opens up the possibility of learning more than simply feeling guilt and letting go of it and disavowing any responsibility for it.

By systematically analyzing transference phenomena and relational re-enactments, psychoanalysis can illuminate ways of being that may either go unnoticed or be submerged in Buddhism—such as a student's idealization of his teachers and his concomitant self-submissiveness (e.g. Tart & Deikman, 1991). In Buddhism this dynamic may remain unexamined, and the student's self-devaluation and deferentiality may never get resolved and may play itself out in various other relationships.

Each school of relational analysis aids Buddhists in understanding more about human relationships. Let me mention several questions that relational analysts could help Buddhists ask:

Object relations oriented analysts remind us to consider: "Who is speaking now and to whom?" Is the meditation teacher who insists that the student follow proper protocol and bow, unwittingly treating the student in the sadistic manner he (the teacher) had been treated by a critical and uncompromising parent as a child? If the student had remained with this teacher and complied with his demands to do bowing practice, might his apparent devotion be enacting a deadly submissive accommodation to an authority he feared and desired to please rather than demonstrating a heartfelt commitment to Zen practice?

Interpersonal analysts elucidate: "What's happening between us (patient and therapist) now?" "How does that replicate key dimensions of the person's life that we are talking about?" and "What can we learn about hidden aspects of ourselves and our relationship?" The ambitious teacher and his self-critical and self-doubting student, for example, could examine how they were both repeating old scenarios rather than relating in a freer and more spontaneous way.

Self-psychologists help us wonder: "What is the state of the self and what form of relatedness and responsiveness is the person searching for now with

me?" The student with the bad back needed a teacher who would be understanding and flexible; the student with massive self-mistrust would have ben-
efitted more from a teacher who helped him grow to trust himself, rather than
exploit him.

Analysts inspired by intersubjectivity theory remind us to wonder: "How
are we co-constructing our relationship now?" "And what recurrent deeply
personal themes are being repeated?" Both the ambitious teacher of Zen and
the student who was all-too-willing to be a doormat co-created the unhealthy
dynamic that characterized their relationship.

Intersubjectivity theory delineates two types of countertransference—
countertransference "conjunction" and countertransference "disjunction"
(Atwood & Stolorow, 1984). In the former, the worldviews of patient and
analyst are so similar that the analyst doesn't think to explore something the
patient says or does that might actually be worth investigating. In the case of
the latter, the world-views of patient and analyst are so different that the analyst simply cannot understand the patient.

Intersubjectivity theory could teach Buddhist teachers to ask: "Am I unem-
pathically engaged with the student because I am either too identified with
them and thereby neglect to examine something that is worthy of further
exploration?" or because "I see things so differently than them that I can't
understand where they are coming from?" The Zen teacher who tried to force
the student with the bad back to bow illustrates the latter. Buddhist teachers
who struggled with substance abuse and rationalized away their own students' struggles illustrate the former.

It might be argued that the scandals in Buddhism are caused by desire
run amok and that the renunciate predilection in Theravadin Buddhism leads
to excessive detachment causing a Freudian "return of the repressed." Buddhism, at least in its classical Theravadin form, has an ambivalent relationship
to emotional life. On the one hand, meditators are counseled to attend to
whatever they experience from terror to love with nonjudgmental acceptance. On the other hand, the purpose of Vipassana meditation is to purify the
mind of "defilements" such as geed, anger, and delusion. Zen and Vajrayana
Buddhism speak of transmuting defilements or poisons—greed, anger, and
delusion—into the three treasures (compassion, love, and wisdom).

Treating certain aspects of our experience as "defilements" can establish an
adversarial relationship to our emotional life in which a dualistic and divided
self engages in an internal "civil war"—involving a presumed superior, right-
eous part of ourselves who tries to get rid of another part of ourselves viewed
as loathsome and expendable.

There are two problems with this diagnosis of the problem of desire run
amok in Buddhist communities: (1) Desire is not the problem, according
to classical Buddhism, thirst (tanha) and grasping are. Tanha, a Pali word
for the thirst that leads to attachment (pratitya-samutpada), is what trips
us—including Buddhist teachers—up. The Buddhist teachers who stole
money from their communities or hungered for power or had sex with

non-consenting students or willingly infected students with AIDS, were trapped in craving not desire.

The second problem with making desire the villain is that in certain schools of Tibetan Buddhism—especially Vajrayana or Tantric Buddhism—desire, like any other aspect of our experience from pain to pleasure, is treated as an essential part of the meditative path; an aid not a hindrance. Passion no less than pain can be a means of accessing the luminous spaciousness and clarity that is ever-present—and without specialized training—obscured. When we are the clarity and compassion of spacious mind even painful or erotic feelings become potential vehicles for awakening. "Tantra" is notoriously difficult to define. It has a long history and a great diversity of beliefs and practices. Tantrism is a general term that is sometimes used by Westerns students of Indian spirituality to designate particular teachings in Hinduism and Buddhism that arose in the early centuries of the common era (Feuerstein, 1996). These teachings cannot be readily summarized because they refer to different, although sometimes overlapping beliefs and practices ranging from the emphasis in certain schools of Tibetan Buddhism on the transmutation of afflictive emotions into the "medicine" of awakening to what Sudhir Kakar (1982) calls the quest for "'wholeness' through psychic androgyny." There is a recognition among many tantric practitioners, that all aspects of our lives—from the body to the feminine principle to our emotions—are potential vehicles for liberation.

But since some of the scandals in Buddhist communities and teacher-student relationships involved Tibetan teachers then either they are incompletely evolved despite the fact that they have presumably been authorized to teach by legitimate authorities, or the teachings themselves need what Derrida (1976) calls a "supplement"—an addition that makes up for a deficiency.

Dancing with Desire: The Practice of Reflective Intimacy

Buddhism is famously known as a middle way or path—sailing a balanced course between the extremes of sensual indulgence and self-mortifying austerities. The Middle Way is a huge contribution to human life, providing a model of balance and wisdom.

The middle path toward emotions and interpersonal relationships would involve neither acting out feelings nor suppressing them. "An American asked the Dalai Lama how one could identify true teachers, and the Dalai Lama said, 'Watch them. See how they behave'" (Tworkov, 1994).

A student admitted to Zen master Suzuki Roshi that she had powerful feelings of love for him, and that it confused her.

"Don't worry," he replied. "You can let yourself have all of the feelings you have for your teacher. That's good. I have enough discipline for both of us" (Chadwick, 2001).

That's a great beginning. But is the middle way enough when emotions overwhelm self-discipline? Since at least Plato we are more aware of how intense feelings often override rationality.

What I call "Reflective Intimacy"—could supplement and enrich Buddhism's middle path toward emotions and relationships.

Most adults experience life indirectly, through a filter of old experience, preconceptions, and second-hand beliefs. It's as if we are stroking a loved one with gloves on.

Zen cultivates heightened intimacy with this moment—a direct and un-self-conscious state of being involving less—or no—separation between the experiencer and the experience. Part of the appeal of Zen to growing numbers of psychoanalysts and their patients may be that this intimacy is deeper than the compromised contact we ordinarily have with the world we live in including in therapy—when we often relate to emotions and people through the filter of what we already know and believe. We speak about anger or depression, for example, but don't really feel the texture of what it means to be resentful or unhappy. That's the role intimacy plays in Reflective Intimacy.

Buddhist teacher Jack Kornfield's interviews with fifty-three Zen masters, [Tibetan] lamas, swamis, and/or their senior students about their sex lives found that for the most part the "'enlightenment' of many of these teachers did not touch their sexuality" (Kornfield, 1993). These teachers, in other words, got caught in cravings that their deep meditation practice—and Buddhist ethical training (sila) didn't transform.

There are, I suspect, at least two reasons for this: It is more difficult to be one with shame or lust than the scent of a lilac or the beauty of a sunset and meditation, as I suggested in Chapters 2 and 3, neglects meaning.

Attempting to merge with emotions is often difficult because they tend to trigger more challenging reactions than nature or inanimate objects. Being one with desire or anger often generates habitual reactions—like attachment or aversion—that emotionally hijack us. We get lost in them or push them away. And then we judge ourselves or blame other people, And when that happens enough times we create a story about ourselves like "I am a person who is angry/depressed/unworthy" which colors—and inhibits direct contact with—the feelings in the present. And then we don't experience our feelings intimately.

Tantric Buddhism provides an indispensable service in teaching practitioners how to open to and feel and befriend emotions and desires. The circle of what we can tolerate and are compassionate toward immeasurably widens. But unless we can also explore meaning, we ignore the messages we receive during meditation and our ordinary lives—in the form of feedback from feelings, images, and symptoms—which contributes to the kind of unconsciousness underwriting the scandals in Buddhism.

Presumably the Zen and Tibetan teachers involved in sexual scandals had erotic feelings before they slept with their students. But instead of these feelings giving them feedback and raising questions they simply acted on them. For example: Did the teacher and his student simply desire each other or might the student have been sexualizing gratitude or testing—and attempting to undermine—the teacher's spiritual authority? Did the student or the teacher feel numb, devitalized, or worthless and want to use sexuality to feel enlivened or validated?

In reflective intimacy, we are intimate with our feelings and desires, by which I mean, we experience the felt sense of the bodily sensations that we conventionally label anxiety/fear/erotic desire and so forth—rather than slot them into the intellectual categories we usually perceive them through. Then we reflect on them and explore their meaning and try to hear what they are communicating. Meaning, as I discussed earlier, often emerges directly and intuitively when we merge with the feelings. And when it doesn't, it can be useful to step back and reflect. That's the reflective aspect of reflective intimacy.

What would have happened if the teachers involved in misconduct became one with these feelings, felt them in their bodies, and noticed what thoughts, feelings and fantasies they triggered. Perhaps some of them might have felt their kinship with and empathy and compassion for their students—a sense that we are both in this together—which might have decreased the chances of simply exploiting them.

And if merging with these feelings didn't organically lead to a sense of connectedness and ethical conduct, then the teachers might have wondered what the feelings might mean about the subjective experience of their students and themselves. The meditation teacher reacting sadistically or erotically to their student could benefit from psychoanalytic attention to reflecting on the meaning of that experience; thus opening up the possibility of using it to help the student—and the teacher—deepen their self-understanding and practice.

Meditation, as I previously suggested, cultivates spaciousness, which helps us build a bigger container in which we can sit with and through a greater range of feelings without the need to suppress them or act them out. Both psychoanalyst Ann Ulanov and Buddhist teacher Charlotte Joko Beck have used this metaphor in describing the fruits of their respective disciplines. Ulanov (2004), for example, speaks of "building a bigger container to make room for all the parts" and Beck (1989) speaks of being "A Bigger Container" and "What is created, what grows, is the amount of life I can hold…"

When we can experience powerful emotions such as vulnerability without getting angry at someone else or trying to escape, for example, we increase the possibilities of understanding what we feel shaky about. Such understanding is the penultimate aspect of living with difficult feelings in a saner way.

When we marry the spaciousness cultivated by meditation and the reflective intimacy encouraged by an integration of the Zen emphasis on being this moment and the psychoanalytic attention to meaning, we could "dance with desire" holding it lightly rather than tightly and using it to learn about ourselves and our students and patients—rather than acting it out, which might lessen the scandals haunting Buddhism.

References

Atwood, George, and Robert Stolorow. *Structures of Subjectivity: Explorations in Psychoanalytic Phenomenology*. Hillsdale, NJ: The Analytic Press, 1984. Page 47.

Baker, Lama Willa. "Breaking the Silence on Sexual Misconduct." *Lion's Roar*, May 19, 2018.

Beck, Charlotte Joko. *Everyday Zen: Love and Work*. New York: Harper, 1989. Page 51.

Boucher, Sandy. *Turning the Wheel: American Women Creating the New Buddhism*. New York: Harper and Row, 1988.

Brown, Daniel and Engler, Jack. "The Stages of Mindfulness Meditation: A Validation Study, Part II: Discussion." In *Transformation of Consciousness: Conventional and Contemplative Perspectives on Development*, edited by Ken Wilber, Jack Engler, and Daniel P. Brown. Boston: Shambhala, 1986. Pages 88–189.

Brown, Daniel P., and Jack Engler. "The Stages of Mindfulness Meditation: A Validation Study." *The Journal of Transpersonal Psychology* 12, no. 2 1980. Page 143.

Butler, Katy. "Encountering the Shadow in Buddhist America." In *Meeting the Shadow: The Hidden Power of the Dark Side of Human Nature*, edited by Connie Zweig and Jeremiah Abrams. New York: Tarcher/Putnam, 1990. Pages 137–147.

Chadwick, David. *To Shine One Corner of the World: Moments with Suzuki Roshi*. New York: Broadway Books, 2001. Page 92.

Derrida, Jacques. *Of Grammatology*. Baltimore, MD: Johns Hopkins University Press, 1976.

Deveaux, Tynette. "Kagyu Thubten Choling (Now Palpung Thubten Choling) addresses sangha about Lama Norlha Rinpoche's sexual misconduct with students." *Lion's Roar*, July 15, 2017.

Ferenczi, Sándor. "The Confusion of Tongues Between Adults and the Child." In *Final Contributions to the Problems and Methods of Psycho-Analysis*. New York: Brunner/Mazel, 1933. Pages 156–167.

Feuerstein, Georg. *The Shambhala Guide to Yoga*. Boston: Shambhala, 1996. Page 128.

Freud, Sigmund. *The Future Prospects of Psycho-Analytic Therapy, Standard Edition XI*. Translated by James Strachey. London: Hogarth Press. 1910. Pages 139–151.

Gleig, Ann and Langenberg, Amy. "Sexual Ethics and Healthy Boundaries in the Wake of Teacher Abuse." *Buddhadharma: The Practitioner's Journal* (Winter, 2023). Page 62.

Goldberg, Natalie. *The Great Failure: My Unexpected Path to Truth*. San Francisco: HarperCollins, 2004. Pages 101–102, 115.

Goleman, Daniel. *Healing Emotions: Conversations with the Dalai Lama on Mindfulness, Emotions, and Health*. Boston: Shambhala, 1997. Page 196.

Kakar, Sudhir. "Tantra and Tantric Healing." In *Shamans, Mystics, and Doctors: A Psychological Inquiry into India and Its Healing Traditions*. Boston: Beacon Press, 1982. Pages 151–190, 163–164.

Kohut, Heinz, and Ernest Wolf. "The Disorders of the Self and Their Treatment: An Outline." *International Journal of Psychoanalysis* 59 197. Pages 413–425.

Kohut, Heinz. *The Analysis of the Self*. New York: International Universities Press, 1971.

Kornfield, Jack. "Sex Lives of the Gurus." *Yoga Journal* 63, no. July/August (1985). Pages 26–28, 66; 259–260.

Kornfield, Jack. *A Path with Heart: A Guide Through the Perils and Promises of Spiritual Life*. New York: Bantam Books, 1993.

Kornfield, Jack. *After the Ecstasy, the Laundry: How the Heart Grows Wise on the Spiritual Path*. New York: Bantam, 2000.

Magid, Barry. *Ordinary Mind: Exploring the Common Ground of Zen and Psychoanalysis*. Boston: Wisdom Publications, 2002. Pages 10–11.

Magid, Barry. *Ending the Pursuit of Happiness: A Zen Guide*. Boston: Wisdom Publications, 2008.

Phillips, Adam. *Terrors and Experts*. Cambridge, MA: Harvard University Press, 1996. Page xvi.

Remski, Matthew. "Survivors of an International Buddhist Cult." *The Walrus*, September 28, 2020.

Ricoeur, Paul. *Freud and Philosophy: An Essay on Interpretation*. New Haven, CT: Yale University Press, 1970.

Rubin, Jeffrey B. *Psychotherapy and Buddhism: Toward an Integration*. New York: Plenum Press, 1996.

Sekida, Katsuki. *The Gateless Gate. In Two Zen Classics: The Gateless Gate and the Blue Cliff Records*. Boston: Shambhala, 2005, Page 118.

Shainberg, Lawrence. *Ambivalent Zen: One Man's Adventures on the Dharma Path*. New York: Vintage Books, 1995. Pages 275, 290–293, 295; 300.

Tart, Charles T., and Arthur Deikman. "Mindfulness, Spiritual Seeking, and Psychotherapy." *Journal of Transpersonal Psychology* 23, no. 1 1991. Pages 29–52.

Tworkov, Helen. *Zen in America*. New York: Kodansha, 1994. Pages 113–143, 157, 237.

Ulanov, Ann Belford. "Psychotherapy and Spirituality." In *Spiritual Aspects of Clinical Work*. Einsiedeln, Switzerland: Daimon Verlag, 2004. Pages 74–108.

Welwood, John. "Spiritual Authority, Genuine and Counterfeit." In *Toward a Psychology of Awakening: Buddhism, Psychotherapy, and the Path of Personal and Spiritual Transformation*. Boston: Shambhala, 2000. Pages 267–281.

7 Practicing Meditative Psychotherapy and Psychoanalysis

There is a natural tendency when we are excited about something to want to dive into it. So, therapists who discover the value of meditation for themselves are prone to want to introduce it into their work.

We need to first focus on bringing it into our lives. The deeper our own practice of meditation, the better able we will be to handle whatever challenges arise—from resistances to meditating to unexpected consequences. We will be able to respond to questions and obstacles our clients encounter based on direct experience.

Protect and Nurture Your Practice

Like athletic fitness, meditative awareness—cultivating concentration and sensory clarity, compassion and equanimity—is a skill that takes practice. There are at least five ways that we can nourish our meditation practice.

One: Build It In

Have you ever wondered why your plans to meditate regularly often fail? Did you ever notice that you are disciplined in certain areas in your life—for example, working out—and not in others? Have you ever been disturbed by the fact that despite your best intentions, your inspired aims to meditate or practice yoga regularly become, at best, distant reminders of yet another botched attempt to achieve goals that you know would be healthy?

We often assume, I think incorrectly, that we are lazy and undisciplined and need more willpower. We then strive with greater intensity to be disciplined and meet our goals, only to fail yet again. And now we feel guilt and shame.

I think I understand why.

I used to meet with my best friend every Monday, Wednesday, and Saturday at noon to play basketball. Factoring in travel, changing, and showering, it took at least two hours. At the same period in my life, I was studying Tai Chi. Practicing the movements I was learning required just ten or fifteen minutes a day. And yet, I practiced irregularly.

DOI: 10.4324/9781003598596-9

Why did I play basketball, which took hours, consistently, and Tai Chi, which took fifteen minutes, erratically?

Clearly, I loved basketball more. But there is another reason, one that offers a clue to being more disciplined and achieving our aspirations. The things we *build into* our lives—that we do unquestioningly—always get done. The things we *fit in*—like my Tai Chi—often are avoided.

When we fit something in—when we plan, for example, to meditate or do yoga sometime today or later this week—we more readily get sidetracked by myriad distractions and interferences. We succumb to fatigue, to competing demands, to simply not feeling like doing it. As a result, we end up failing to achieve our aims.

However, when we build into our lives what matters to us, there is an established structure to help us meet our aspirations. This plan—which demarcates a necessity and a time—is the boundary that supports our goals. When we truly perceive something as essential, like eating, showering, or sleeping, we make sure to do it. We set up routines that incorporate these activities, and our routines are safeguards against the forces that divert us from our path. There is less room for loopholes and excuses. After building meditation and qigong into my daily life—making a time and place for them in my schedule and a commitment to myself to do them no matter how I felt or what competing demands existed—it became much easier to organize my day so that both got done.

If you really want to deepen your practice of meditation, you need to build it into your life by making it an established, unquestioned part of your daily routine. This can take several forms: regularly scheduled sitting and walking meditation; periodic intensive retreats; and practice amid life—mindfulness during daily tasks such as eating and washing, speaking and working.

Paying heightened attention to tasks we take for granted—brushing our teeth, ingesting food, and doing the dishes—and to transitions in daily life (walking up the steps or to the store or out to the car) is an important way to develop a continuity of awareness, which nurtures and deepens our practice.

Two: Treat Life as the Dojo

Many meditators and students and teachers of yoga have what I call "segregated" practice. They diligently meditate or perform asanas, but neither activity really touches their regular lives, what they do "off the mat." They are mindful on the cushion and heedless elsewhere. We solidify our practice by bringing it into daily life, as well as by building it in. Some martial arts teachers emphasize that life is the dojo (Homma, 1990) or training center, by which they mean that nothing we experience is outside our practice, from difficult emotions to challenging relationships.

Mindfulness during moments when we are upset is immensely helpful in strengthening our practice and developing focus and balance of mind.

Ordinarily our patterns of relating to ourselves and other people remain taken for granted, unconscious, and "hidden in plain sight." Treat crisis as a potential teacher. In times of difficulties or calamity—when we are "triggered"— our habitual patterns and conflicts are not only closer to the surface and more evident, but more amenable to being seen and transformed. When we are curious about why we overreacted or underreacted to some situation, for example, it can be a doorway into our deeper conditioning.

Three: Practice Intimacy

A meditation teacher hurt his hand just before beginning his own retreat. He was in a lot of pain. For the first day and a half of his self-retreat, his practice mostly consisted of continuously labeling his agony "pain" whenever it arose. The pain persisted for a day and a half, until he noticed that he was doing this in order to "keep it at arm's length," at which point the pain dissolved.

In the same way, most of us also keep life at bay. We relate to it from a distance. We practice intimacy—a notion that derived from my Zen training— when we engage life more directly and less self-consciously. A patient who was a Buddhist teacher was annoyed and fed up with one of his students who didn't understand why the teacher wasn't "happier." The teacher had an agonizing childhood filled with both abuse and neglect. But he also relished life. The song of the birds, the laughter of children, and the kindness of strangers were essential to his experience of the world.

"Because of trauma you carry an immense burden that you may not have shed," I said. "But you do cherish life. Perhaps your student correctly pinpointed your melancholy and is very disappointed that you are not perfect and ideal."

"I completely agree," the teacher said.

"What if you stay connected to your feelings of hurt and rejection, and then use the conflict with your student as an opportunity to examine what he expects from you—that you must be perfect and can't be human—and how such expectations shape and perhaps limit his own practice?" I asked.

"I think I'll wait till I calm down a little and do that," he replied.

A week later, he said that he had spoken in this vein to his student, and the conflict was lessened. Their bond, which had been meaningful to both of them, was reestablished.

Practicing intimacy can take many forms, from trying to stay connected to painful emotional states to examining interpersonal tensions and conflicts that we ordinarily would avoid or blame on other people. You can begin this practice by trying to pay attention to how your body is feeling several times a day. Are you depleted or energized? Do you need to stretch or move or rest?

Usually, we try to avoid what we don't like. Practicing intimacy is the courage and willingness to dive into life and engage the whole shebang, including the messy aspects.

Four: Bring Practice to Life

One of the greatest challenges most meditators must grapple with is how to bring practice into their lives, into the way they relate to other people and care for themselves—or don't. While the major Buddhist meditative traditions agree on the importance of this goal, the monastic traditions of Buddhism in Asia—the soil from which Buddhism arose and developed—do not provide readily adaptable models for integrating practice into secular lay life, which is the major concern of practitioners outside monasteries. From a monastic point of view, feelings, the body, and relationships are causes of enormous suffering and distraction, and segregating Buddhist practice from these aspects of ordinary lay life makes individual liberation more possible. A remarkable—but largely unremarked upon—phenomenon is that Western Buddhism tends to be a lay practice. While Mahayana Buddhism, with its focus on compassionate engagement with people and the world, challenged and broadened classical Buddhism's individualistic ideal, incorporating practice into daily life has not been fully delineated even within this tradition.

"Bringing our practice to life" means two separate and interrelated things: making it relate to our actual lives and come alive.

There are at least three ways we can achieve these two goals. First, we can try to make daily life meditative. Second, we strive to live our values and embody our ethics in how we live. And third, we must be sure to explore neglected areas of our lives, including emotions, our bodies, and our relationships.

When I teach, I often suggest that we change the word "meditation" to "meditative." Meditation pursued mindlessly is not meditative; anything, however, can be meditative if done wholeheartedly and with full attention. This includes washing, dressing, writing an email, doing the laundry, packing a suitcase, driving a car, riding the subway, or handling interpersonal and ethical conflicts.

In *The Art of Flourishing,* I describe the gap for most of us between what we claim to value and how we actually live. Detecting and closing that gap is a crucial aspect of living a contemplative life.

There's a tension I have observed over the years in meditation practice. Instructions emphasize paying nonjudgmental attention to whatever arises. This is a wonderful tool for therapists and clients alike. However, many meditators complain of the way certain crucial areas of their lives—emotions, the body, and relationships—are often neglected and not sufficiently addressed in their practice.

There are two ways to remedy this. The first is to stop what you are doing several times during the day and check in with yourself. Take a moment to notice how you are feeling. The second is to engage in what I call "stopping on a dime" practice. Whenever you feel under the grip of intense emotions or catch yourself engaging in repetitive behavior or thoughtless speech—gossip, lies, or slanderous talk—stop for a moment and try to mindfully observe the gaps between your life and your practice and endeavor to live your higher values.

Five: Incorporate Feedback

Modify your efforts to bring your practice to life based on feedback you receive. Ask yourself: Am I becoming more empathic and understanding? More kindhearted and less self-critical? Wiser and more patient with other people and myself? Be willing to revise your efforts and direction based on what you learn. After noticing that I was much more accepting of other people than myself, I placed more emphasis during meditation on working with self-judgment, which dramatically lessened it, and deepened my practice.

Principles of Integration

Integrating meditation into psychotherapy can take various forms—from meditators (including Buddhist teachers) who seek psychotherapy to therapists who introduce Buddhist principles or practices (like walking or sitting meditation or lovingkindness practices) into treatment. What is crucial when meditative practice is initiated by the therapist—when, for example, I suggested that the client who was overwhelmed in a session do walking meditation—is the clinician's centeredness and clarity. That's one reason I recommended in the previous section that the therapist's first priority is bringing meditation into his or her own life.

Integrating meditation into psychotherapy depends on two elements: the attitude and receptivity of the analysand and the sensitivity of the analyst. When I am focused and centered, and my mind is alert and pliable—a state I call "expanded inner space" in my book *The Art of Flourishing*—then I am more attuned to my clients and what they need.

Most people assume that introducing meditation into therapy is linked to diagnosis. The principle seems to be that the more disturbed the patient, the less likely it is that meditation can be introduced. In my experience, the issues are more complex. I have seen "neurotics" who don't take to meditation and so-called "psychotics" who do.

P-I-A-N-O-S is an acronym for the principles I use to integrate meditation into therapy. It stands for: Play the Edge and Individualize, Interest, Adapt and Evolve, Necessity, Opportunity, Study Your Impact.

One: Play the Edge

My first yoga teacher, Joel Kramer, developed a principle he called "playing the edge." Stand with your feet spread shoulder-width apart. Gently bend down toward your toes. The edge is the place of intensity without pain. At your physical edge, you are challenged, but not injured. We also have emotional edges—experiences or actions that are difficult for us, like speaking up in a class, but not injurious. Emotional edges are those places that may scare us but lead to growth and transformation.

A Buddhist student of mine meditated for fifteen or twenty minutes a day and wanted to meditate longer. "Many people experience that more practice may cultivate greater concentration and equanimity," I said, "but sometimes meditators can push too hard and then stop meditating altogether. What if you played the edge and found a place in between cruise control and being overwhelmed?"

"That sounds great," she replied.

The "edge" will be different for each one of us, and we must each individualize our practice to find what works best for us. For a long time, I began my day with a lengthy period of sitting meditation. I assumed that this was positive for me. That is, until I met Lobsang Rapgay, a practitioner of Tibetan medicine, psychologist, and author, and former deputy secretary to the Dalai Lama. He recommended that it was healthier for me to move at the beginning of the day because I had a phlegmatic physical constitution. Over time, I realized that beginning my day with qigong or hatha yoga—mindful physical movement—was much more energizing and clarifying than waking up and immediately doing sitting meditation. Somebody with a different constitution might benefit from meditating first and then moving.

Healing modalities must be individualized, and must challenge us, but not beyond our limits. Since everyone is unique, the way meditation is combined with psychotherapy can't be standardized ahead of time, nor can it remain a static process.

Two: Interest

Everyone is unique. While we know this on a theoretical level, we often forget it in practice. There is something reassuring about a standard-brand approach to psychotherapy, meditation, or to living, but it eclipses the way we are all different.

We live with much greater passion and focus and joy when we allow ourselves to discover and take seriously what interests and inspires us, whether singing or gardening, walking through the park or doing yoga. Notice what you keep daydreaming about doing, or what you used to love, but gradually drifted away from because of work or habit.

When we bring this same attitude to meditation practice—making our practice a reflection of what inspires us—our motivation to practice deepens and our practice becomes more effortless and joyful. When meditators take seriously what they are curious about and interested in, their meditation has more passion. So, ask students of meditation or meditating clients what inspires them and create meditative practices that reflect that. Many years ago, I taught a class called "Bringing Practice to Life" at a Buddhist center. Many of the students, who ranged in age from mid-twenties to early sixties, were very interested in meditative practices that placed greater emphasis on connecting with and learning to handle challenging emotions so that became a central focus.

Three: Adapt and Evolve

Practicing meditative psychotherapy demands that we look honestly at the results of what we do and make changes accordingly. The client's well-being is, of course, more important than our pride or belief in our favorite theories or practices. Successful therapy may require us to alter what we are doing based on feedback from the client.

A female therapist with a severe trauma history meditated irregularly. We explored this in our sessions, but the pattern persisted—until we realized that she avoided meditation at home because it brought up disturbing memories and painful emotions. We decided to meditate together during a session. We discovered that not only did new insights emerge, but she was also eventually able to return to meditating on her own at home.

Four: Necessity

Some years ago, I was teaching meditation and yogic breathing to the Michigan Group Psychotherapy Association. Our meetings took place on the first floor of a hotel. Just before the beginning of our Saturday morning workshop, a large marching band was practicing outside. I quickly calculated that we shouldn't begin with focusing on quieting the mind through using the breath because it might be too difficult for the participants to do this with so much noise nearby. Because of the unexpected necessity of practicing amid a great deal of racket, I suggested that we make sound the focus of our initial meditation practice. At first the noise was disruptive because we heard it more clearly. But eventually it was no longer a distraction once we joined it, instead of fighting against it.

Such unexpected "necessities" demand that we shift focus to take them into account.

Five: Opportunity

A man with a great deal of equanimity had a memory while meditating of a troubling interaction with a parent. At first, he simply let go of it. But when it returned, he remembered what I had said to him about being alert to unexpected opportunities during his practice. As he leaned into the memory of his conversation with his father anger arose. Remaining with his rage at being mistreated, he contacted a well of sadness. Anger rarely arose in his daily meditation practice. But by attending to it a doorway opened up into deeper intimacy with and understanding of himself.

Six: Study Impact

One objection to attempting to integrate meditation into psychotherapy might be that it violates a sacred shibboleth of therapy, namely the therapist's "neutrality." The quest for neutrality has much to recommend it. It protects the patient's autonomy and increases the chances that therapy will not be governed by the subjective biases and blind spots of the clinician. But neutrality is a myth. Some patients will experience a therapist who attempts to be neutral and anonymous as professional, safe, and objective. Clients who were scarred by an emotionally cold and withholding parent might feel rejected and insignificant.

Once therapists stop trying to be neutral, the natural question that arises is: "What is my impact?" Therapists who introduce meditation into psychotherapy need to be honest with themselves about its effect. Did it make the client feel empowered or more submissive? Does meditation aid them in soothing themselves under duress or prove to them that they are inadequate and can't even remain concentrated for a few seconds in a row?

The Marriage of Meditation and Meaning

Psychoanalysis and Buddhism have become engaged in the second decade of the new millennium. If they marry and have a more intimate and egalitarian relationship, characterized by mutual respect, an awareness of differences, and a willingness and capacity to learn from each other, the child of their union—*meditative psychoanalysis*—could offer profound solace and guidance to a world that has lost its way. Meditative psychoanalysis can provide realistic hope and accessible pathways to fostering abiding change.

Reference

Homma, Gaku. *Aikido for Life*. Berkeley, CA: North Atlantic Books, 1990. Page 3.

Part III

Meditative Psychoanalysis in the World

Love and Hate, Transience and a Well-Lived Life

8   Fools in Love
Zen and Intimacy

"I can't write about Zen and love because I have been a fool in love," my Zen teacher once said to me.

"We all have been," I replied. "You can still write about love," I added, "because you taught me that a Zen approach would involve, at least in part, embracing—being intimate with—one's foolishness."

Sex, money, and in-laws might seem, at first glance, like the locus of irrationality in romance. But until recently, I was certain that the chief obstacle to intimacy—and the major cause of our foolishness—was the tendency most of us have to try to *win*, rather than to *understand*, which renders our partners opponents we attempt to defeat or thwart, rather than friends we strive to empathize with. Winning in a relationship is a losing proposition.

I now believe that successful intimacy is so fraught and elusive because it involves a task that few of us are prepared for—namely, integrating two different emotional worlds. Worlds of emotional experience are enormously complex and multi-faceted. They contain core values and vital passions, psychological strengths and emotional wounds, unacknowledged hopes and recurrent fears, secret wishes and hidden expectations. When two such universes come in contact, something new can be born that lessens our isolation, gives our lives meaning, and leaves us immeasurably enriched. But worlds of experience can also clash, collide, and cancel each other out because of conflicting values, irreconcilable goals, or an inability to respect and skillfully navigate differences. Getting emotional universes to harmonize over time and weather the challenges that confront significant relationships is an art that few of us have mastered.

How do we avoid being fools in love? We can't. But perhaps with practice we can lessen our self-blindness, operate more wisely, and co-create more loving unions.

The first step is to become intimate with our foolishness. We have several misconceptions about love and intimacy. We assume, without really thinking about it, that love is an instantaneous and ecstatic feeling. "I looked across the room and knew they were the one," people say. What exactly did they know, I wonder? That the other person was physically attractive or well-dressed,

DOI: 10.4324/9781003598596-11

gazed at them in a way that felt penetrating or inviting? Since they knew nothing about the person's character, interests, or values—whether they were compassionate or sadistic, committed to health or self-neglectful, trustworthy or parasitic—the attraction was fairly mechanical and self-centered. The person across the room simply fit their image of what they desired to have or to be—a necessary yet wholly insufficient basis for a stable, loving relationship.

The second misconception about love is that it is a *feeling a person possesses*—glorious and ecstatic. One of the wisest insights of contemporary psychoanalysis is that emotions, which include love, are better thought of as having a context and co-created by two people rather than the internal possession of one. From that perspective, the rapture of love is based on an *environment* that a couple creates and sustains—or neglects and subverts.

This realization opens up a very different way of thinking about love than contemporary culture encourages. Lasting intimacy—a close and enduring relationship with someone we adore who cherishes us—is a marathon that requires training, not a sprint that takes a few moments. Reconciling, integrating, and expanding the worlds of experience of both members of a couple is a practice that demands patience and self-awareness, empathy and flexibility, resourcefulness and humor—qualities that are not in abundance today, when we live at a frenzied pace, are bombarded with information, and feel demoralized about the state of the world.

Self-care is the foundation of intimacy. Investing in the relationship begins with taking care of ourselves. There is no intimacy with another person without self-care, cultivating what helps us flourish: discovering our passions, finding our purpose, understanding and handling our feelings wisely, and living authentically.

The final stage and culmination of self-care is intimacy. The practice of intimacy is immeasurably enriched by engaging in more direct contact with life as it is. At their best, Zen and psychoanalysis both facilitate this. Both promote the capacity to be present and open to the full range of our experiences. In addition, Zen and psychoanalysis foster self-knowledge, intimacy with oneself, and compassion, three crucial ingredients in integrating worlds of experience. To love, you need to be aware of your talents and limitations—especially the obstacles you bring to the relationship—and be comfortable in your own skin and with your partner's less-than-perfect-humanness.

Meditation and psychotherapy help us be more at home in our lives. Both traditions also help release us from the suffocating grip of thinking our way of life is the only valid one. This frees us to stretch ourselves to accommodate the worlds of our partners, instead of dismissing, assimilating, and reducing them into our own.

Like a garden, an intimate relationship has weeds and pests; it needs tending, or it languishes. A relationship must be continually maintained—watered and fed, weeded and composted. We need to make tending to the relationship a priority, deepen empathy for our partner's experience, sensitively express our feelings and needs, and work mindfully with conflicts and imbalances in power. We also must find a place to house and compassionately work with disappointment, hurt, and anger. A loving relationship is a home for idealization and passion, but it is also a breeding ground for disillusionment and resentment. The beloved inevitably activates early wounds and unconscious patterns of unhealthy relating.

But the loved one can also serve as an invaluable resource in self-healing and personal transformation. We are attracted to those who emotionally resemble significant people from our past. If they didn't, we probably wouldn't be drawn to them. But they also offer the promise of healing unfinished emotional wounds. To the extent that old patterns are repeated, and each partner treats the other person as their parents did, they remain stuck in previous and restrictive conditioning. When the promise the partner offers of being a more benign and healing presence is actualized, there is growth and transformation. And then the relationship becomes a place where the couple not only puts out psychological fires but can dream together about—and strive to actualize—a better life.

Wholeheartedly engaging the relationship when it is difficult and fails to conform to our idealized and romanticized images of how it should be is vital. It can be terrifying, painful, and exhausting when the hoped-for sanctuary of the relationship becomes an emotional minefield or prison. It is not surprising that contempt, self-doubt, and despair sometimes arise. But at such moments, we must give ourselves permission to have our feelings even if they are scary to contemplate or unsettling to express. The greatest threat to the integrity of the relationship is not having disturbing feelings, but dismissing them, which usually leads to physical or psychological symptoms or illnesses and emotional distress.

In an ideal situation, our feelings and the discontent they represent are compassionately held, witnessed, and validated by our partner, which is indispensable in healing. Without that understanding and confirmation, we all tend to hold on to the feelings as a kind of silent memorial to our unwitnessed pain. But when our feelings are met with empathy, it's an invitation for understanding and healing—perhaps by heartfelt apologies and wiser responses that not only repair the damage that has been done but open up new pathways for emotional intimacy in the present.

None of us are experts about love, but we can all lessen—although not eliminate—our foolishness and expand our capacity to open to unfamiliar worlds of experience and even create new ones that surpass anything we had previously imagined.

When separate psychological universes intersect, there can be enriching and transformative cross-pollination—or annihilating collisions. Mutually respectful relationships that integrate apparent opposites—like self-care and altruism, insight and action, security and risk—create new worlds that are composed of elements of each person's old ones, but which transcend and enrich them. The relationship becomes a refuge, not just from a speeding and distracted and demoralized world that has lost its way, but from our own doubts and fears and emotional vulnerabilities. From that sanctuary, we can more easily befriend both the wounded and shameful parts of ourselves and the hidden potentials that have rarely emerged. Not only do we become more than we were, but we also grow into who we want to be. We become freer to create a new life and future beyond anything we could have imagined, which is of inestimable value in a world in which love is endangered and a precarious achievement.

9 Hate Hides Where We Are Hurting

Psychoanalytic-Meditative Contemplations

The most significant threat to America may lie within. When COVID is a nightmarish memory of a ghastly cultural plague, I fear the social virus of hate infecting America—hateful speech, violent actions, and stunning and heartbreaking heartlessness—will continue to haunt, bewilder, and assault us. Hatred seems to be arising with greater frequency in every area of our world from politics and religion to on-line and on the road.

It is easy to miss the mark when thinking about this topic. Amid a raging culture war, replete with a great deal of demonizing and scapegoating, people tend to be divided between sympathizers who condone recent hate-based bigotry, misogyny, and violence and opponents who abhor it. But neither those who rationalize and extol hate or despise it illuminate its sources—or the emotional fall-out. This chapter presents a psychotherapeutic-meditative approach to hate that will not only shed light on the causes and the pathway to transformation, but may provide unsuspected insight about how we might begin to relate to hate more wisely inside and outside our offices and meditative/spiritual communities.

Let's begin by considering some vignettes and moments in psychotherapy involving hate—by which I mean loathing or detesting, despising or shunning.

"I hate you; I hope you die," a man in his early thirties said to his father when he was eighteen.

"For many years I hated my father," a famous psychologist who has done groundbreaking research on emotions admitted. "He was a cruel man, insulting," he adds, "physically abusive (Ekman, 2008)…Hatred poisoned my overall character, facilitating anger whenever I was blocked by someone…My hatred for my father…made me into a person easily angered toward anyone, about anything."

Many years ago, I treated a woman who was emotionally scarred by early trauma and had a lot of free-floating rage. She had little self-awareness and less self-control and was verbally abusive in a way I never encountered before or since. Seemingly out of nowhere she would launch into blistering attacks and scream at me continuously, which frequently left me feeling brutalized, shell-shocked, and exhausted.

DOI: 10.4324/9781003598596-12

The eminent psychoanalyst D.W. Winnicott (1947/1978) tells the following story about his own hate toward a patient:

> During the second world war a boy of nine came to a hostel for evacuated children, sent from London…because of truancy. I hoped to give him some treatment during his stay in the hostel, but his symptom won, and he ran away as he had always done from everywhere since the age of six when he first ran away from home. However, I had established contact with him in one interview in which I could see and interpret through a drawing of his that in running away he was unconsciously saving the inside of his home and preserving his mother from assault, as well as trying to get away from his own inner world which was full of persecutors.
>
> I was not very surprised when he turned up in the police station very near my home. This was one of the few police stations that did not know him intimately. My wife very generously took him in and kept him for three months, three months of hell. He was the most lovable and most maddening of children, often stark staring mad. But fortunately, we knew what to expect. We dealt with the first phase by giving him complete freedom and a shilling whenever he went out. He had only to ring up and we fetched him from whatever police station had taken charge of him.
>
> Soon the expected change-over occurred, the truancy symptom turned round, and the boy started dramatizing the assault on the inside. It was really a whole-time job for the two of us together.
>
> The important thing is the way in which the evolution of the boy's personality engendered hate in me, and what I did about it. (1947/1978).

"I hate myself—I'm a failure, loathsome and unlovable," a highly competent and creative middle-aged man informs me.

Another man hated Jews and people of color who he claimed were trying to extinguish him and the white race. He played a large role in the planning of the murder of a (Jewish) talk-radio host and drove the getaway car.

"Hatred saved my life," a talented therapist and devoted Tibetan Buddhist informed me many years ago. "It helped me protest against my father's savage cruelty and survive a gruesome childhood."

"What do I do with the rage I feel toward some patients?" a supervisee who was a Buddhist, asked me several years ago.

Human beings can be kind and compassionate, they can also be hateful and sadistic.

Why do we hate other people—or ourselves? What is the impact? What can we do about it?

Hatred or ill-will, was, for the Buddha (2004), one of three root afflictive emotions. And it never ceases by hatred. Freud (1915) linked hate to thwarted love; Melanie Klein (1957/1975) to envy—"The angry feeling that another person possesses and enjoys something desirable—the envious impulse being to take it away or to spoil it"; D.W. Winnicott (1969) to the quest for self-articulation and differentiation; Otto Kernberg to malignant narcissism; and Heinz Kohut (1972) to threats to the stability, integrity, or sense of self.

In my experience, hate doesn't have a single or definitive source, although there may be one common denominator that illuminates it: namely, hate hides where we are emotionally hurting. "I imagine one of the reasons people cling to their hates so stubbornly," James Baldwin (1955) aptly notes, "is because they sense, once hate is gone, they will be forced to deal with pain."

Some people feel hate when blocked or stymied, humiliated or endangered—in the face of feeling forsaken, invisible, and forgotten, as increasing numbers of people report on each side of the seemingly unbridgeable political divide in the US and throughout the world. Hate arises in others when the emotional worlds they inhabit—or their sense of entitlement—have been challenged or violated. When other people represent a threat to how we see the world it can generate hate. Trauma may cause hate. And so may impending death as Dylan Thomas (2017) put it so eloquently when he wrote: "Rage, rage against the dying of the light."

We know hate harms and undermines—our own immunity and our relationships with other people—but if truth be told it also can be energizing. Let's briefly consider both. Hate simplifies a complex world—creating a reductionistic, binary universe of us versus them: "You're for us or against us" that distorts, pathologizes, and scapegoats gender and race, religion and political viewpoints that are different than our own. We are then convinced that the people who are opposed to us are deluded and disgraceful. Hate harms them and us emotionally, physically, and interpersonally, clouding clear perception and sound judgment, compassion and the urge for connection often leading to troubling (sometimes unspeakable) cruelties.

Hate and fury can also sometimes affirm us (Eigen, 1986), by pumping us up and reducing—or hiding—our emotional vulnerability. Hate in the form of outrage about social oppression or injustice can fuel and mobilize action, as it did in the Civil Rights and Women's Movement—and more recently the LGBTQ Movement.

Eastern meditative and Western psychotherapeutic traditions have grappled with challenging emotions like hate from different—but perhaps ultimately synergistic—perspectives. Eastern meditative traditions alert us to possibilities of heightened focus and clarity, compassion and wisdom—especially ethical perspectives that can potentially enrich Western psychotherapeutic ones. Western therapeutic traditions—especially psychoanalysis—illuminate the sources and meaning of hate, which can enrich meditative perspectives.

A man is hired to assassinate Gandhi. He attends a talk that Gandhi is giving. The would-be assassin is so taken with the power of Gandhi's ethical presence and teachings that he goes up to Gandhi afterwards, prostrates himself and tells Gandhi his original intention. Imagine a person hired to kill you admitted this to you and knelt down in front of you. What would you feel? *What would you say?*

Gandhi's response?

"What are you going to tell your boss about your failed plan?" At a moment when most people—and I suspect this includes psychotherapists—might be enraged about the murderous intentions that have been admitted to them, Gandhi empathizes with the new trouble the would-be assassin is in.

Eastern meditative approaches to hate can teach Western psychology about possibilities for compassion and wisdom that transcend ordinary conceptions of mental health. That's their first gift.

To experience the second gift of the East I invite you to think briefly about an experience of hatred—toward another person or yourself—and try this short meditation practice.

Sit in a comfortable position, if you can, back upright and relaxed. Since we are going to be breathing through our nose it is best to close your mouth. Pull the air to the back of your throat on the inhale. On the exhale, gently press your abdomen toward your spine without any strain. If the breath is comfortable, please feel free to continue with it. If it isn't, open your mouth and breathe normally.

Now pay attention to sound. See if you can open to it, hear it, let it wash over you. If your mind wanders, which happens to even experienced meditators, try to notice it and return without judgment to hearing sound.

Consider the experience of hate that you wrote down before we did some yogic breathing and Buddhist meditation. Is it any different? Do you feel it more? Are you any more intimate with it?

Emotions like hate are not only central to human existence, but they are also complex—often more multidimensional than meets the eye/I. Hostility or contempt can mask feeling fearful or vulnerable, shameful or loathsome. Emotions like hate are also enormously difficult to handle—and they can all-too-easily hijack us. Psychoanalysis is one of the best approaches to understanding the intricacy of emotional life and challenging feelings like hate (Rubin, 2017).

But psychoanalysis all-often-often biologizes such passions and neglects their relational and existential influences. Therapists also sometimes approach emotions like hate in an experience-distant, rationalistically oriented, emotionally unintimate way that unconsciously keeps them at arm's length and eclipses the lived experience of them. When therapists try to figure out what a feeling means, we all-too-often fall into a fatal trap. We recognize a familiar emotion like hostility and slot it into a pre-existing system of meaning and significance: "There's my anger or rage." At first such labeling seems clarifying and ends the sense of confusion. But that initial relief obscures that instead of staying with the experience that has just arisen—say a whiff or subtle flavor of hurt or sadness, irritation or resentment—and working inductively, from the inside out, to amplify and understand it, we unwittingly move away from it by attempting to link it with a recognizable feeling. At that moment we are alienated from the actual texture of what we have just lived through. That's the first problem with the psychoanalytic approach to feelings.

Here's the second. I'm on a cross-country flight after a psychoanalytic conference, sitting near the window. Next to me are an affable woman and her infant son. On the other side of the aisle is a highly intelligent psychoanalytic colleague. The baby cries most of the trip. My colleague gets progressively more disturbed. I open to the sound of the baby and try to experience it as directly as I can, instead of fighting or bemoaning it. While I like quietude as much as the next person, the practice of meditation has taught me that when I open to the noise instead of resisting it, it intrudes less forcefully upon inner experience. Initially, the sounds are more vivid, and I hear them more intensely. Soon after, I have space from them and don't feel enveloped or troubled by them. Toward the end of the trip, I am standing next to my colleague in the aisle. "How did you handle the noise? It's driving me crazy," she said. My initial surprise lessened when I realized that she approached the crying very differently than I did.

The second difficulty with the psychoanalytic approach to feelings is the absence of a methodology to handle the peremptory nature of emotions. Feelings arise seemingly unbidden and assault us, flood us, hijack us, or cause us to withdraw and shut down, as thinkers from Aristotle to Ekman (2008) have recognized. Without meditative resources, we tend to become embedded in our experience and we have more trouble identifying, metabolizing, reflecting upon, modulating, or skillfully responding to intense feelings.

Meditation, paying careful attention without judgment or interference to what we experience moment-by-moment, provides a corrective to the lacuna in the psychoanalytic method: It helps one gain direct contact with emotions so we can feel their texture, creating space from, titrating our exposure to, and helping us gain a clearer perspective on them. This is invaluable. But there is a fundamental omission in the meditative approach to emotions like hate. Eastern meditative perspectives neglect *meaning,* as we explored in the second and third chapters (Rubin, 2018; 2026).

It is easier to denounce evil doers than to strive to understand them. Hate, like madness, has a story to tell. And understanding where people are coming from that hate—which doesn't preclude holding them morally accountable for sexism, racism, and violence—is crucial and often more important than techniques or remedies that momentarily pacify the feelings—perhaps including yoga and meditation—while neglecting the source. It is difficult to address malevolence that we don't comprehend.

A Deeper Look

Let's look further into some of the illustrative vignettes I presented at the beginning of this chapter with perspectives gleaned from a Meditative Psychoanalytic perspective.

Meditative practices, as I suggested earlier—and we hopefully got a glimpse of when we meditated together—cultivate heightened focus and clarity, equanimity and compassion. That's indispensable for listening to and noticing what is around and inside of us. It also lessens self-criticism and cultivates a capacity for sitting with feelings without denying them, pushing them away, or projecting them onto other people.

As wonderful as meditation is, it isn't focused on or designed for decoding or translating meaning, as I highlighted earlier. At the first Buddhist retreat I ever attended in the late 1970s, a wealth of unconscious insights emerged as I meditated for hours a day. "What do I do with these insights?" I asked one of the teachers. "Don't do anything," he replied, "just let go." Letting go has great value a lot of the time. It is a powerful way of not falling victim to two illnesses that pervade Western culture and the human mind, namely ruminating about the past and fantasizing about the future. Both interfere with embodying and appreciating the only life we have, which is what is happening now.

But letting go has a shadow side that all-too-many meditators may miss—it can cause us to prematurely detach from what we need to pay attention to. And that is a petri dish for growing self-blindness and self-imprisonment. It is an important aspect of scandals in spiritual communities and obstacles in one's meditation practice.

Let's return to the vignettes.

The question of how a therapist manages being hated arose for me with the first two vignettes I am going to reflect on.

"I feel like hitting you over the head with this chair," a man I'll call Roger said to me many years ago during a session several months into treatment.

"What holds you back?" I asked.

"My feelings are like nuclear waste," he replied.

"They could contaminate the world?"

I learned that when Roger was eighteen, he tried for the first time to separate from his dad, an overbearing, intellectual man who was devoted to socialist politics and "high" culture. Roger's efforts to carve out his own life put him increasingly at odds with his father. But his dad's approval still meant the world to him. While Roger longed for the appreciation of his remote father, he felt compelled to have his own voice. "I hate you I hope you die," Roger said to his dad one day in anger. His father was devastated and began crying. Roger felt horrible.

When our parents are devastated by our feelings, we develop distorted ideas about ourselves. We may think we are despicable or burdensome. Or poisonous.

After his father's crushing reaction to his expression of hostility, Roger developed the deadly idea that he was "toxic," and other people were excessively fragile. He repressed his natural aggression, and he began to see the world as if it was like his father—incapable of handling his genuine feelings. So, he began living in a highly controlled and excessively timid way, terrified of damaging other people through his words. But this often resulted in rage emerging unexpectedly.

The safety of our relationship eventually provided an anchor for Roger and me to explore his horrendous past—especially the invalidating experiences and massive absence of attunement to his feelings and needs, which drove him crazy and undermined his belief in his own personal reality. This caused paralyzing self-doubt and was annihilating. Delusions developed, which were a desperate attempt at self-healing and symbolically expressed how he had been endangered. His delusions were emotional snapshots of traumas he had endured but which no one had ever acknowledged or understood. Feeling that aliens were stealing the encyclopedia he was reading and that rays were being beamed into the bus he was riding masterfully evoked the twin feelings of being robbed of vital knowledge and of being taken over by an outside "alien" force that was oblivious to his own wishes and needs. When he told his mother that the roof was leaking and needed to be fixed, for example, she ignored him and read *Finnegans Wake* as water dripped on the rug nearby.

Over the course of our work together, Roger made profound strides. Understanding the roots and current impact of his delusions helped him gradually develop a fragile faith in the validity of his own experience. As his self-trust deepened, the voices that assaulted him lessened. He began feeling more real and alive. He moved into his own apartment, bought a car that he used to get to work and to our tri-weekly sessions, learned several computer languages, got a job working in a college admissions office, and slowly developed several relationships of value and substance.

Roger taught me many things over our ten years of working together. Chief among them was the inestimable importance of valuing human experience and searching for the emotional wisdom underlying even apparently bizarre and crazy behavior. My patients—even the most obviously troubled ones—have repeatedly shown me that their words and actions make sense; that there is a secret meaning they are striving for that I must struggle to understand. So when I hear something that seems harmful or self-destructive such as hate or "delusions," suicidal ideation or self-mutilation, I try to find the underlying meaning, which makes it possible to reach people who feel lost and alone and locked in a private world of torment.

One of the gravest dangers afflicting our culture in general and the field of mental health in particular is the assault on human subjectivity, the decreasing interest in honoring and valuing people's experience. In the craze to map the brain and prescribe pills for psychological disorders, the field of mental health is not only getting hijacked, but also losing its soul (Rubin, 2026).

As I suggested in Chapter 1, the willingness to bear witness to the full spectrum of feelings people undergo is crucial in healing.

The question of how a therapist manages being hated or hating arose for me with the client who screamed at me (and a client I recently heard about from a Jewish colleague, who proudly displayed his KKK tattoos). I tried everything I knew to manage the situation with the former, but nothing worked.

I explored whether she felt hurt, let down, or endangered by me and whether I was enraging her. I wondered if she was trying to help me feel what she had endured at the hands of an abuser. Perhaps she was eschewing human connections—while desperately hungering for them—to avoid being retraumatized. Empathy, kindness, understanding, setting limits, and letting her know her impact on me failed to stem her verbal assaults. They—and both her and my suffering—persisted.

After I weathered several of these excruciating assaults, I learned that she had seen and sued several therapists including a trusted colleague's friend, an esteemed practitioner. My colleague earnestly informed me that I was doing good work because she hadn't yet sued me, but that reassurance, as you can imagine, didn't make it easier to sit through our sessions or the multiple vicious screaming messages from this bright and creative professor on my answering machine in between sessions.

When we think about hate we often think about terrorism, invasions, and contemporary political divisions. Hate is within and between us—toward other people AND ourselves. Many of us have been overtaken by forces within that turn against us and we don't/can't control. A person may be at war with themselves.

"The important thing…is the way in which the evolution of the boy's personality engendered hate in me, and what I did about it" Winnicott (1947/1978) said about the truant he and his wife took in. "Did I hit him?" Winnicott said. "The answer is no, I never hit. But *I should have had to have done so if I had not known all about my hate and if I had not let him know about it too.*" [Winnicott (1947/1978); my italics].

In recent years my own work has moved increasingly outward beyond the consulting room into the larger world that our lives are embedded in. I have written psychobiographies of Trump and a prominent white extremist. My last vignette will hopefully shed light on hate-in-the-world.

The best theories we have outside psychotherapy about the causes of hate don't get to the source of the problem. I learned this when I studied the actual life and the psychology of a key figure in domestic terrorism. The Chicago Project on Security and Threats (CPOST) has studied the demographics of the "377 Americans, from 250 counties in 44 states, arrested or charged in the Capital attack," as Charles Pierce notes in the April 6, 2021, issue of *Esquire*. Based on two additional independent surveys in February and March, including a National Opinion Research Council survey, CPOST concluded that fear of the "Great Replacement," rather than economic insecurity, was at the root of the rage. The "Great Replacement" theory—the notion that Whites are being displaced and replaced because of mass immigration and low birth rates resulting in rapidly rising, non-White populations—certainly sheds light on some elements of fury among White people. And yet, despite the fact that it has "achieved iconic status," as Pierce notes, it also hides a deeper source of resentment. A unifying thread and rallying cry of white supremacists is the belief in "white genocide." It is hard for those who don't share this conviction to understand how neo-Nazis and Ku Klux Klan members, militias and Aryan survivalists came to assume that white people are threatened with extinction by mass immigration, intermarriage, and "forced assimilation." In the case of David Lane, who popularized this belief, fears of extinction seem based on a childhood trauma, an unconscious fear from the past, instilled by a white father who terrorized and endangered him and his mother and brother, not people of color.

Lane, a neo-Nazi and convicted felon, was the poster child for twentieth-century white nationalism. He was best known on the right for penning "14 Words," arguably the most renowned white supremacist slogan: "We must secure the existence of our people and a future for White children." "The single greatest issue of our time," according to Lane, is "racial survival." "America is the murderer of the white race," Lane wrote in "Tri-Colored Treason."

White people living in fear of "extermination" is an old story in American history. "Some seem to see today anti-Christ in Catholicism, and in Jews, international plotters of the Protocol; and in 'the rising tide of color,' a threat to all civilization and human culture," W.E.B. Dubois wrote in *Black Reconstructionism,* published in 1935. Speaking of Lothrop Stoddard's 1920 *The Rising Tide of Color: The Threat Against White World-Supremacy*, F. Scott Fitzgerald's character Tom Buchanan in *The Great Gatsby* (1925) favorably embraced Stoddard's view: "Well, it's a fine book, everybody ought to read it. The idea is if we don't look out the white race will be—will be utterly submerged. It's all scientific stuff; it's been proved."

It was David Lane who took these views and brought them to a wider audience.

David Lane was born on November 2, 1938, in Woten, Iowa. "My only memory of my mother is as a tall, severe woman who never smiled," he writes in his autobiography. His father "seems to have been a drunk, a scoundrel, and a low-life of the worst kind… particularly when drunk, a truly despicable creature. He sold my mother to his buddies and to strangers for booze money. He beat the entire family, often with a razor strap."

And then there was this heartbreaking recollection:

In 1942, the family was living in a room over a hardware store in Woten, Iowa. With no wood for the stove, which provided the only heat during cold northern Iowa winters, my brother Roger [two years David's senior] started a fire in the stove with available materials, including the razor strap. For this my father beat him so badly that he broke Roger's eardrums and he was deaf for the rest of his life. For this reason, he was never adopted from the orphanage where we all ended up.

After David's father left his family in 1942, he mistreated another young wife, and "a brother of the new victim smashed his head in with a hammer, and Gerd went to wherever trash goes after death." In 1943, David was "adopted out of the orphanage" by a "doctrinaire, fundamentalist, Lutheran minister from the old school. He had a personality which practically no one could bear." His new mother "was an enigma... To this day I cannot fathom how she could abandon her own talents and ego to traipse about the country with someone I considered an obnoxious buffoon."

Something murderous and unspeakable was done to David Lane and his family...*by his father*.

When your father beats you and abandons you, you are made to feel annihilated and erased, worthless and unlovable. What makes dreadful events traumatic, notes psychoanalyst Robert Stolorow (2007) in *Trauma and Human Existence*, is not the incident alone, but the absence of an emotional home for one's feelings. Not only did David Lane go through a devastating experience, but he also had to face it by himself. And that intensified the psychological damage.

The nightmare his father put David through gave him a life mission: save white children from being extinguished. But in some ways, the extinction David feared in the future, "The Death of The White Race is neither imaginary nor far off in the distant future" he wrote—already *happened*, but in *his past*: the emotional "*murder*" he had undergone at home. The British psychoanalyst D.W. Winnicott (1963/1989) suggested that a fear of breakdown—or death (I'd add soul murder)—was a breakdown that happened in the person's past but was not remembered and the unremembered memory was preserved in the fear projected into the future.

"The future for White children" David Lane yearned to "secure"—and that has inspired thousands of white supremacists—was one his father annihilated in him. By blaming blacks and immigrants, Jews and women for the "extermination" he didn't realize he had experienced at the hands of his father and aligning with a community of embittered men who stoked his anger rather than empathized with his pain, David distanced himself from the real source of his agony, took his father off the hook, and scapegoated innocent people. Racializing emotional extinction—attributing fears of obliteration to nameless people of color David Lane never met—warded off the unspeakable and unbearable nightmare that his father had psychologically obliterated him. In so doing, Lane unwittingly insured that his primal wound was not addressed, and his trauma would be foisted on the world.

Not everyone who is traumatized becomes an extremist. Some torched souls respond to their agony by becoming therapists or loving parents, poets or professors, martial artists or painters, rather than perpetuators of violence or abuse. It's likely not possible to claim that all white supremacists were once traumatized. But I think we can reasonably speculate that some kind of ghastly unconscious trauma may live in possibly many people in the white supremacist movement.

Combatting homegrown extremists and hate is a complex problem demanding multi-pronged strategies. Understanding the emotional sources of their fear and alienation, which the example of David Lane suggests, is emotional trauma close to home, as well as being culturally supplanted and marginalized, is crucial. So is countering propaganda, decreasing the cultural and economic conditions that contribute to radicalization, creating laws relating to domestic terrorism, and granting more legal authority to monitor domestic hate speech. Getting in touch with emotional horror, although devastating, even shattering, perhaps affords the best hope of lessening the possibility that such traumas are so frequently revisited on innocent people in the world.

The Implications

"In this world hostilities are never appeased by hostility," the Buddha (2004) aptly noted in the *Dhammapada*, a core text on Buddhist ethics. "But by the absence of hostility are they appeased," he added. What we have today is a destructive mutually escalating cycle of hate begetting more hate. While hate is never cured by hate, loving our enemies seems today like a wonderful ideal that most people find enormously difficult to embody—and not a panacea.

"It demands great spiritual resilience not to hate the hater whose foot is on your neck, and an even greater miracle of perception and charity not to teach your child to hate," James Baldwin (1962) writes in a "Letter from a Region in My Mind" in the *New Yorker* November 17, 1962). I hold out hope that maybe sometimes if we could meet the hater—outside or inside—with empathy and equanimity, instead of contempt and volatility, something unexpected might happen. At first our attempt at understanding and compassion—our implicit communication that they are not deplorable—might make them feel *worse.* If they are not hateful then the hateful ways that they were treated would feel more betraying, sickening, and demoralizing. "If I am not truly despicable, how could this have been done to me?" is the way they might conceive of it. But if together we could live through that disillusionment and grief a space might open up for some new sense of self to be born. And that could be a seedbed of a massive change of direction. You see this in Christian Picciolini's (2017) autobiography, *White American Youth: My Descent into America's Most Violent Hate Movement—and How I Got Out.* Picciolini, a former American extremist and co-founder of *Life After Hate*, an organization devoted to help people extricate themselves from violent and extremist organizations, was a massively alienated young man who was recruited at fourteen to join a neo-Nazi Skinhead group. His life spiraled out of control as he became more centrally involved in hate groups.

As he was met with acceptance by people very different than himself in the record store he owned, he gradually realized that the apparent community and identity he thought he had as a hate-based extremist was a lie. And this helped him to change direction and work to free casualties of the white supremacist movement from the emotional prisons that enslaved them.

Hate is sometimes intractable and non-participation, not love, may be the route one has to go. A colleague recently told me the following story. A patient who had been abused by his father and unprotected by his mother took off his cap and turned his head so that his KKK tattoo was directly visible to her, a Jewish therapist. She felt hated but thought she should be able to handle it. She explored what he was trying to say to her and wondered what he was trying to let her know—or make her feel—about what he silently endured alone. Was he unconsciously giving her a window into the horror that he had undergone as a boy and as a young man? None of these efforts at understanding aided them in finding a place of co-existence in a world that harms by hating or shunning.

Sometimes understanding—or love—is enough like with the man who wanted to hit me over the head with his chair or the middle-aged man with self-hatred. Sometimes perhaps it is not. I am linking hate to emotional hurt. What if someone is taught to hate from a young age? Sometimes we can breathe or meditate our way through—like with the woman who screamed at me during and in between sessions. At other times we try our best and remain devoted to help the souls in pain we work with, but need to try not to play out—and amplify and perpetuate—the hateful cycle or invitation. I was sitting in my office in between sessions meditating. I heard a new couple yelling at each other in the waiting room. As I meditated, what emerged was a thought about the possible meaning of their animosity, the second pillar of meditative psychoanalysis.

As they shrieked at each other in my office a few minutes later their overt contempt for each other was intense and disturbing. I felt like I was witnessing two snipers trying to take each other out. I was also convinced that they had a hidden agenda and were "playing to the audience."

"No," I said, when they were in my office.

"No to what?" they asked.

"No to the secret set up we find ourselves in" (which I only realized because of the insight revealed by meditative-psychoanalytic listening).

"Which is what?" one of them asked.

"To join you in court as a character witness—a slanderer—against your spouse. I try to help couples make it or separate as humanely as possible. I will not be conscripted to participate in a "litigious war with you in court."

The third pillar of meditative psychoanalysis, liberated intimacy, enabled me to relate to this apparent conundrum with greater self-reflectiveness and creativity.

They were silent and looked like actors without a script.

Since the analyst in meditative psychoanalysis is like an emotional jazz improviser, let's riff on what I did and said.

Here's what I would say now:

"Under your rage and hatred may lie disillusionment and demoralization, fear and hurt. Facing emotional darkness can be a bridge to a path that heals. Your relationship might feel over—you may be 'done.' But I wonder if we could take very seriously what troubles each of you, understand the way your worlds might be colliding, and see if together we could forge another way".

References

Baldwin, James. "Me and My House." *Harper's Magazine*, November 1955.

Baldwin, James. "Letter from a Region in My Mind." *The New Yorker*, November 17, 1962. https://www.newyorker.com.

Buddha, Siddhartha Gautama. *Dhammapada*. Translated by Glenn Wallis. New York: The Modern Library, 2004. Page 4.

Ekman, Paul, ed. *Emotional Awareness: A Conversation Between the Dalai Lama & Paul Ekman*. New York: Henry Holt & Company, 2008. Pages 133, 136.

Eigen, Michael. "Hate." In *The Psychotic Core*. New York: Jason Aronson, 1986. Pages 169–213.

Freud, Sigmund. "Instincts and Their Vicissitudes." In *The Standard Edition of the Complete Psychological Works of Sigmund Freud, Standard Edition*, 14. London: Hogarth Press, 1915. Pages 109–140.

Klein, Melanie. *Envy and Gratitude & Other Works 1946–1963*. New York: Dell Publishing Company, 1957/1975. Pages 176–235.

Kohut, Heinz. "Thoughts on Narcissism and Narcissistic Rage." In *Self Psychology and the Humanities*. New York: W.W. Norton & Company, 1972/1985. Pages 124–160.

Picciolini, Christian. *White American Youth: My Descent into America's Most Violent Hate Movement—and How I Got Out*. New York: Hachette Books, 2017.

Pierce, Charles. "A New Study Draws a Line from January 6 to Charlottesville." https://www.esquire.com/news-politics/politics/a36040222/robert-pape-cpost-report-january-6-insurrection/April 6, 2021.

Rubin, Jeffrey B. "Emotional Flourishing: Cultivating Self-Awareness, Empathy, and Wise Action." In *The Art of Flourishing: A Guide to Mindfulness, Self-Care, and Love in a Chaotic World*. New York: Skyhorse, 2017. Pages 84–111.

Rubin, Jeffrey B. "The Marriage of Intimacy and Meaning: A Psychoanalytic-Meditative Approach to Passions and Feelings." In *Psychoanalytic Perspectives on Passion: Meanings and Manifestations in the Clinical Setting and Beyond*, edited by Brent Willock, Rebecca Curtis, and Lori Bohm. New York: Routledge, 2018. Pages 95–100.

Rubin, Jeffrey B. *Psychotherapy Case Studies: Escaping the Prison You Didn't Know You Were In*. New York: Routledge, 2026.

Stolorow, Robert D. *Trauma and Human Existence: Autobiographical, Psychoanalytic, and Philosophical Reflections*. New York: Routledge, 2007.

Thomas, Dylan. *The Poems of Dylan Thomas*. New York: New Directions, 2017.

Winnicott, Donald W. "Hate in the Counter-Transference." In *Through Paediatrics to Psycho-Analysis*. London: Hogarth Press, 1945/1978. Pages 194–200.

Winnicott, Donald W. "Fear of Breakdown." In *Psycho-Analytic Explorations*. Cambridge, MA: Harvard University Press. 1963/1989. Pages 87–95.

Winnicott, Donald W. "The Use of an Object and Relating Through Identifications." In *Playing and Reality*. London: Tavistock Publications, 1969/1971. Pages 86–94.

10 Death, Transience, and an Ethics of Mortality

During a summer walk through a beautiful countryside with a famous young poet (assumed to be Rainer Maria Rilke) and a taciturn friend (assumed to be Lou Andreas-Salomé), Freud (1915) noted that the poet "admired the beauty of the scene," but felt no joy in it because he was disturbed that the beauty was "fated to extinction" (Freud 1915) and was thus "shorn of its worth by the transience which was its doom."

Freud (1915) disagreed with the poet's view that the "transience of what is beautiful" (Freud 1915) should interfere with our joy of it: "A flower that blossoms only for a single night does not seem to us on that account less lovely" (1915), he writes; a perspective that seems consistent with Buddhism. The "evanescence of the human form and face," Freud adds, "lends them a fresh charm" (1915).

"The proneness to decay" of beauty gives rise two reactions, Freud (1915) writes, "the aching despondency" of Rilke, or a "rebellion" (Freud 1915) against its transience and a wish for "immortality" (Freud 1915), which is illustrated by the notion of rebirth, a speculative doctrine in Buddhism that reflected the world view of Buddha's time, but has not to my knowledge been proved or demonstrated. In response to my questioning of rebirth—Shinzen Young, a visionary Buddhist teacher of mine, informed me that he had interviewed fifty Zen masters about the topic and none had an experience of, or belief in, the doctrine.

Both Rilke's sadness and the desire for immortality are, in Freud's view, defensive solutions to disturbing facets of life and a protection against, and a resistance to, mourning.

A great seer, Asita, foresaw in a trance that a king's son had a great part to play in healing suffering and leading people to salvation. The king shielded his son from distractions, sensual pleasures, and anything that could perturb his mind. One day the prince, feeling trapped, snuck away from the sheltered palace and ventured out with his attendant. He confronted old age in the form of an elderly, toothless, and haggard man, sickness, and death. The prince was stunned and deeply troubled by these sights. His charioteer explained to him that old age was not rare, but happens to everyone (Arnold, 1969). The prince ordered the charioteer to immediately turn around and return to the

DOI: 10.4324/9781003598596-13

kingdom. That evening the man we know as the Buddha abandoned his family and initiated a spiritual quest to get to the bottom of and find a way around the reality of suffering.

"I teach one thing and one thing only: suffering and the end of suffering," the Buddha is reputed to have said. Buddhist meditation was the technique the Buddha developed to handle the existential misery and trauma he encountered when he witnessed, for the first time, old age, suffering, and death. Profoundly distressed, even haunted, by the reality and inevitably of aging, misery, and mortality, he produced a set of teachings and practices whose central focus was eliminating the agony that traumatized him. The Buddha's response suggests an attempt to evade transience and grief, rather than confront and mourn it.

A well-known writer on Buddhism and meditation told me many years ago that after his divorce, meditation helped him anesthetize his pain and grief. Concentrating his mind during meditation kept his loss and sadness at bay, which he recognized unnecessarily prolonged the mourning process—because he never grieved his loss, it took longer to get over it.

When he became interested in truly experiencing and learning from his sadness, loneliness, and fear, rather than anesthetizing himself or getting rid of his feelings by prematurely detaching from them, a new world opened up.

Toward an Ethics of Mortality

"I have all the time in the world," a confident, aggressive, thirty-something financial manager I'll call ET (for "Mr. Endless Time") told me, his therapist, in his first session many years ago. "I have plenty of time to settle down and be more disciplined and responsible. For now, I'd rather have fun, play the field, and enjoy my life."

Yes and no, I thought.

He comes from hardy stock, and if he is fortunate—and careful—he may live a long life and have a great deal of time. But life—with all its transience and loss—keeps reminding us that while most of us operate as if we have endless time, we don't.

Jorge Luis Borges' (1949/2004) short story "The Immortal" is about a group of people who live forever. At first, a life without the passage of time—or death—seems wonderful. All the time in the world to reach their goals, enjoy the fruits of their efforts, and soak in the pleasures of the world.

But the denizens of Borges' city of immortals live in a gilded nightmare. Lulled by immortality and the fantasy of permanence, they feel no urgency to do anything because it can always be done later. Indifference, passivity, and complacency flourish, and investment in one's own fate and the plight of other people wanes.

"Death makes men precious and pathetic," wrote Borges. "[E]very act they execute may be their last; there is not a face that is not on the verge of dissolving like a face in a dream. Everything among the mortals has the value of the irretrievable and the perilous. Among the Immortals, on the other hand... nothing can happen only once, nothing is preciously precarious."

And so, nothing is important or essential.

We cling to the fantasy of endless time for various reasons: from fear of our own deaths to wanting to deny or minimize possibilities that will never be. If we have all the time in the world, loves and opportunities lost—from singing opera to playing center field for the Yankees—might be magically redeemed.

Twenty years after I originally met Mr. Endless Time, he unexpectedly returned to therapy. He had come in only for a consultation that first time around, but he shared enough about himself in that session for me to remember how assured and self-possessed he had appeared. When we reconnected, we spent our sessions mapping the contours of the panic that afflicted him. It wasn't caused by the alienating and unfulfilling work he toiled at or the hair loss, middle-aged paunch, and swollen eyes he now exhibited. We understood his nameless dread only after we illuminated a faintly recalled nightmare that had left him unsettled and confused. "There's a murky orange object and a ticking sound," he reported.

"Anything come to mind about either?" I asked.

"There's an orange clock covered with ants in Salvador Dali's painting *The Persistence of Memory,*" he said.

There's also a melting pocket watch in it. "Anything else come to mind about the orange clock, Dali, or ants?" I asked.

"Time," he said.

My patient had a pensive expression and seemed to be searching for something, so I remained silent.

"Time stands still for no one," he continued. "It melts away like butter in a pan. It's gone before you know it."

In subsequent sessions he was sadder and more vulnerable. Gone was the jaunty, the-universe-is-my-amusement-park attitude. He now understood that he did *not* have all the time in the world. He lived in an in-between time worse than those lonely and soul-crunching sleepless, middle-of-the-night hours: no longer oblivious to time's passage; not yet reconciled to whatever finite time remained.

Eventually Mr. Endless Time stopped denying the finiteness of time. And he no longer descended into fatalism and resignation. The reality of not having all the time in the world helped him treat his mortality—and his life—more seriously. Aware of the restrictions of time, my chastened client dived more wholeheartedly into what he was doing and felt more urgency about leaving a mark on the world he formerly saw as "an endless breast to drink from." Mr. Endless Time now used the time he had more urgently and carefully and no longer took his existence for granted.

When we, like him, let go of the fantasy of having all the time in the world, we awaken from a trance. Facing our transience head on, which psychoanalysis—and meditation practice without the doctrine of rebirth—helps us to do; opens the door to what my friend Joel Kramer called an "ethics of mortality": cherishing and embracing transitory life precisely because it is "Once for each thing. Just once, no more. And we too,/just once. And never again," as Rilke (1923/1982) elsewhere wrote. In an "Ethics of Mortality" life's finitude would inspire and galvanize us, instead of leaching life of value. "That it will never come again is what makes life so sweet," wrote Emily Dickinson (1961). Then we could attempt to create meaning, savor our existence, and forge significant emotional relationships out of the circumscribed life we have.

References

Arnold, Edwin. *The Light of India*. Adyar, India: Theosophical Publishing House, 1969. Page 39.

Borges, Jorge Luis. "The Immortal." In *The Aleph and Other Stories*. New York: Penguin, 1949/2004. Page 15, Pages 3–19.

Dickinson, Emily. "741." In *The Complete Poems of Emily Dickinson*, edited by Thomas H. Johnson. Boston: Little, Brown and Company, 1961. Page 706.

Freud, Sigmund. "On Transience." In *The Standard Edition of the Complete Psychological Works of Sigmund Freud, Standard Edition*, 14. London: Hogarth Press, 1915. Pages 305–306.

Rilke, Rainer Maria. "The Ninth [Duino] Elegy." In Selected Poetry of Rainer Maria Rilke, translated by Stephen Mitchell. New York: Random House, 1923/1982. Page 199.

11 A Well-Lived Life
Psychoanalytic and Buddhist Contributions

Psychoanalysis and Buddhism each have something rare and vital to contribute to the challenges and difficulties of living in our world. The capacity of these two wisdom traditions to help us live with greater self-awareness and self-acceptance, care and compassion, morality and freedom is essential in a world permeated by self-blindness and (self)-hatred, powerlessness and alienation. This chapter explores what light psychoanalysis and Buddhism can shed on a life well-lived.

First, I shall explore why illuminating the nature of the good life is important to psychoanalysis. Then I'll suggest why psychoanalysis is in a unique position to elucidate the well-lived life. This is followed by diverse and divergent psychoanalytic perspectives—including classical psychoanalytic, Jungian, Kleinian, object relational, interpersonal, self-psychological, and intersubjective—on the good life. Implications for such issues as the nature of self, morality, and freedom are offered. Buddhist contributions drawn from Theravadin, Zen, and Tibetan traditions will be interspersed throughout, which offer a counterpart to psychoanalytic ones, thereby illuminating hidden presuppositions of psychoanalysis as well as helping us raise new questions and gain novel insights about the good life.

Given psychoanalysis' avowed commitment to moral neutrality it may sound strange at first to speak of psychoanalysis and the good life. The good life or the full life is not something that psychoanalysis usually is or should be prescriptive about. One of the many virtues of psychoanalysis is that unlike ancient spiritual traditions or contemporary psycho-spiritual writings, it does not legislate or provide formulaic answers to the question of "how one should live one's life." There are many virtues to such as attitude including the minimization of coercive external impositions, the protection of the patient's autonomy, and the openness to many different ways of living.

The neglect of health in psychoanalysis and its reluctance in engaging values makes psychoanalysis seem like an unpromising candidate for illuminating the well-lived life. In fact, psychoanalysis may not appear to offer anything to this topic unless we approach it psychoanalytically, by which I mean, reading psychoanalysis against its grain; questioning standard interpretations of psychoanalysis (even by psychoanalysts); searching for latent as

DOI: 10.4324/9781003598596-14

opposed to manifest meanings and implications in psychoanalytic formulations, and treating what is not said by psychoanalysts as sometimes as meaningful as what is said. To take up a "Freudian" attitude toward psychoanalysis itself is to be interested in unconscious facets of psychoanalytic theory and practice (Rubin, 1998). The psychoanalytic legacy about the good life is contained not in any explicit instructions about how we should live and may only be germinally present in analytic writings. There are implications about a life well-lived in psychoanalytic writings and uses to which psychoanalytic perspectives can be put that analytic thinkers may not always have consciously intended and of which they may not always be aware. Since the full implications are not always evident, they may often not be integrated into one's way of living.

It is often assumed outside psychoanalysis—occasionally even within it (e.g. Molino & Ware, 2001)—that psychoanalysis is normalizing, by which I mean, a form of social control and conformity. But psychoanalysis is transgressive and de-normalizing as well as constraining (Breger, 1981, Rubin, 1998). Psychoanalysis exemplifies its conservativeness when it knows too much beforehand about what is successful human development or how psychoanalytic treatment proceeds. When this happens then the patient is placed in a Procrustean bed and unsuspected possibilities for treatment and the person's growth and development are narrowed. But psychoanalysis illustrates its liberatory potential when it challenges its own absolute authority and transforms or overcomes and extends the normative standards that it establishes. More fertile and suggestive perspectives on the good life emerge when psychoanalysis questions and destabilizes its own authority rather than when it establishes universalistic models which patients are slotted into.

While psychoanalysis has usefully eschewed a prescriptive perspective on values, implicit in psychoanalysis are a variety of suggestive perspectives on a life well-lived. Despite the commitment to helping parents find their own answers to questions about how to live, psychoanalysis is not, nor could it ever be, neutral about such topics. Embedded in psychoanalysis are all sorts of conscious and unconscious notions about the kinds of values and lives that are worth living. In this chapter, I will attempt to explore and make more conscious what W.H. Auden (1962) termed, the "dream of Eden," the visions of the good life that psychoanalysis values. Rendering them more conscious gives us the opportunity to be more reflective about them, which could contribute to living a fuller life. It also opens up tacit knowledge encoded within psychoanalysis which may remain buried and thus not accessible for enriching living if it remains undetected.

The quest to live a good life has a venerable history. The central concern for Lao Tzu, Buddha, Socrates, Aristotle, Epicurus, Jesus, the Prophets, Montaigne, Thoreau, Nietzsche, Marx, and Schweitzer among others—those individuals that Fromm (1995) calls "masters of living"—was how humans should live. Two ways of thinking about this broad and important topic dominate contemporary thinking: a secular, materialistic ideal and a "spiritual" one.

François Rabelais ends his satirical masterpiece Gargantua with the construction of the Abbey of Thélème. In Thélème wealth, happiness, and pleasure are the goals of life. In our world the good life is often linked to similar, hedonistic images: conjuring up a variety of associations including "having it all"; the unlimited freedom to purchase and accumulate; the ability to obtain ceaseless pleasure, luxury, and ease; the capacity and power to shape one's life and to segregate oneself from noxious external impingements including any unwanted obligations and constraints. The popular media—the internet and movies, television and magazines—exalt this kind of life. A large percentage of people in our society find this goal enormously compelling. Even those who decry the vacuousness of this ideal often judge themselves according to whether they actually embody it. Believing, with AT&T that "It's all within your reach," the unconscious (sometimes conscious) assumption for the vast majority of people is that if they achieve these goals then they will be happy.

Yet obviously even the very wealthy experience a great deal of alienation, emptiness, and stress-related disorders and the feeling that 'there has to be something more.' The Dalai Lama (Gyatso, 1999) points out that poorer nations have sanitation related illnesses, while more highly urbanized, industrialized nations such as the United States have a greater preponderance of stress-related ones. That there is not a direct correlation between financial wealth and emotional health is probably not news to any analyst who has listened to the disillusionment and sometimes despair of their wealthier patients.

"Having it all" or attempting to achieve it does not necessarily constitute a life well-lived and in fact is sometimes an obstacle to it. This is not surprising. The most remarkable feature of the Abbey of Thélème, after all, is its thick walls, not its hedonism and sensuous delight. From inside the Abbey of Thélème one has privacy and is secluded from the outside world. But one also cannot see the "other side." Good fences, claims Robert Frost, make good neighbors. They also make good prisons. The wall at Thélème incarcerates its inhabitants as well as keeps outsiders out.

There is a countervailing perspective on the good life that is increasingly popular in our world, namely the "spiritual" point of view. Spiritual perspectives on the good life cannot be put in a monolithic formula. But they do seem to share several compatible features which offer a powerful counter-pressure to the ceaseless pursuit of wealth and leisure such as the attempt to discover and embody our essential, authentic self; the idealization of selflessness; and the belief in an uncontaminated realm "beyond ego" that it is humanly possible to experience. It is often asserted that one could then permanently and irreversibly experience such enlightenment. Pursuing this goal is presumed to lead to living authentically and purely. An important facet of this is an other-centered ethics which establishes self-centeredness as a villain and is assumed to eradicate egocentricity and promote balanced and sane living (Gyatso, 1999).

There are a growing number of people who find these and related spiritual ideals compelling. But the rash of scandals in spiritual communities in recent years involving rampant egocentricity and complete lack of moral accountability, a topic we explored in Chapter 6, "Dancing with Desire," cast gave doubt on spiritual images of the good life and the ideal of selflessness. As do the problems with abuse of power that numerous Buddhist teachers have been involved in.

Psychoanalysis complicates secular and spiritual pictures of the well-lived life. While many contemplative traditions acknowledge that humans confront resistances to growth and have great difficulty changing, they tend to lack the comprehensive understanding of and systematic approach to unconsciousness that psychoanalysis offers, a topic we addressed in Chapter 2, "Deepening Listening."

The unconscious, what Jung thought of as the unknown as it lives in and through us and shapes us, confirms the fallibility of the analyst and the guru. Our inability to know ourselves completely means that there will always be areas of both ourselves and the interpersonal and external world that are opaque and that remain to be explored and discovered. The spiritual ideal of achieving perfect and complete knowledge of ourselves is thus more of a romantic wish-fulfilment that has seduced spiritual seekers than a reality that we can directly experience ourselves.

Psychoanalysis critiques the psychological moralities of contemplative traditions because of the way they decomplexify psychological life and ethics. Part of this is due to the fact that contemplative traditions neglect human development; the ubiquity of self-deception; the shaping role of the past (the way our individual and family histories close down as well as open up certain possibilities; the fact that our past shapes and delimits how we care for or neglect ourselves and relate to others and the world); and the stubbornness of character, transference, and unconsciousness (Rubin, 1996). Contemplative traditions do not address the way intentions and actions may have multiple unconscious meanings and functions. Altruism in a spiritual practitioner may hide vanity and piousness. Self-denigration may masquerade as spiritual asceticism. And humility can be fueled by a sense of non-entitlement or fear of competition no less than a recognition of the suffering and limitation generated by an excessively possessive relation to a theory, material object, or psychological or spiritual practice.

The problems with both contemplative and secular conceptions of a life well-lived leave us adrift; lacking a guiding vision or a framework for action. It is a central claim of this chapter that psychoanalysis and Buddhism might be an unexpected resource in this area, making a significant contribution to this topic.

Psychoanalysis seems, at first glance, ill-equipped for elucidating the good life because of its tragic world view (with its focus on illness not health), its emphasis on the isolated, unencumbered individual, and its commitment to moral neutrality. Psychoanalysis is underwritten by a "tragic" world view, that is, a recognition of the inescapable mysteries, dilemmas, and afflictions pervading human existence (Schafer, 1976). Religious consolations are quixotic in the tragic vision. Analysts such as Ferenczi, Jung, Horney, Fromm, Winnicott, Eigen and Phillips, among others, have embraced a more affirmative and less tragic conception of the world.

Deriving from and intimately connected to its tragic world view; psychoanalysis is a psychology of illness that neglects health and creativity, intimacy and spirituality (Rank, Fromm, Milner, Eigen, and Rubin, are exceptions to the generalization). Psychoanalysis, as Winnicott (1971) aptly noted, has "yet to tackle the question of *what life itself is about*" apart from illness. The *Standard Edition* of the works of Freud, for example, contain over 400 entries for neurosis and not one for health. Because psychoanalysis has focused on pathology it tends to conceive of health, as Freud's "pathography" of Leonardo illustrates, as an absence of illness rather than the presence of well-being. To read psychoanalytic accounts of the "ends of analysis"—personal integration; heightened reality testing; the capacity to "love and work"; developing ego strength; cultivating the ability for self-reflection and self-analysis—is to understand why artists and spiritual seekers, among others, all too often believe that there is more on earth (I don't about heaven) than psychoanalytic accounts of the good life suggest. Contemplative perspectives on the human condition suggest that psychoanalysis contributes to suffering by its tragic and secular worldview and by systematically underestimating human possibilities for healing and health. It is thus not surprising that the concept of the good life rarely appears in the psychoanalytic literature.

Illuminating the nature of the Good Life is important for psychoanalysis for at least two reasons: the first is clinical, the second is cultural. Psychoanalysis is not value neutral. The analyst has a vision of the good life even if they do not consciously formulate it and consciously subscribes to the view that they should have no vision apart from that of applying neutrally the analytic method. To know when to terminate a treatment the analyst must have an image of cure; to know what a cure is one must have a vision of the good life. These visions shape our daily work in hidden ways that are no less important because they are unconscious. In fact, they are more formative because they are hidden.

The second reason the topic of the good life is important has to do with psychoanalysis' problematic standing in and relation to the contemporary world. We live in two senses in a demoralized world. Many people feel discouraged, beaten down, and disenchanted. Second, we live in an age where morality is the exception; where hedonism reigns in most domains of human conduct. Elected officials, religious figures, executives, the media, entertainers, and professional athletes, do what enhances the self and are without scruples or concern for their impact on others. In a world that resembles a moral free-for-all; where anything goes; where everything can be deconstructed and debunked from reason to revelation, people are left with no foundations or guiding direction for action. Many people then feel cast drift. What fills the breach is egocentricity, hedonism, popular psycho-spiritual quick fixes and self-anesthetizing behavior. Is it surprising that we feel moral malaise?

Psychoanalysis is in a good position to illuminate the good life for at least three reasons: (1) Psychoanalysis is a sanctuary from the cognitive saturation, emotional disconnection, and pressure to live flattened lives that permeates our culture (Rubin, 1998). This provides an emotionally intimate and relatively non-impinging context for exploring such questions of ultimate concern as how one should live. (2) Psychoanalysis is in a position to illuminate the good life because it has access to depths of human subjectivity that are not explored anywhere else in daily life. Psychoanalysis appreciates unconsciousness which religious and spiritual disciplines all too often neglect. (3) Psychoanalysis, unlike most postmodernist discourse, is critical yet reconstructive, demystifying yet affirmative. Psychoanalysts question the authority humans often irrationally invest in others, yet they do not deny expertise. Psychoanalysts recognize that there is no objectivity, but they do not usher in a disabling nihilism. Psychoanalysts throw out the baby of self-mastery, yet they do not drain the bathwater of self-awareness (Rubin, 1998).

And yet, despite psychoanalysis' potential to illuminate the good life, one could search in vain for psychoanalytic citations on this topic. Erich Fromm (1947, 1995), Leslie Farber (1976), and myself (Rubin, 2004) are in a distinct minority in addressing this important and neglected topic. There are at least five reasons this topic has been neglected in psychoanalysis:

1 Hitching its star to science was one important way that psychoanalysis tried to legitimate itself in a psychoanalytically inhospitable world. Neutrality was central to the self-image of science. The legacy of neutrality made analysts queasy about the "anxiety of influence." It is thus normal analytic practice for the analyst to refrain from expressing any ideas about the Good Life to the patient.
2 Novick (1997) has comprehensively illuminated psychoanalysts' resistance to termination and the terminal phase of treatment. Since it is in this phase of treatment that reflections on cure and the good life may explicitly play the most central role; neglecting this facet of the treatment meant that the issue of health was neglected by psychoanalysts.
3 The fully analyzed patient (or analyst!) is more readily viewed as a fiction in contemporary psychoanalysis. Recognizing the illusoriness of perfectionistic ideals of a "complete analysis," we analysts may neglect the topic of health.
4 With its tragic worldview, psychoanalysis is a psychology of illness; focusing on what goes wrong in development. The best humans could achieve, according to Freud (Breuer & Freud, 1895), was to transform "neurotic misery into common unhappiness."
5 According to Freud, suffering is inevitable because of the inherent tension between our biological nature, especially our instincts, and the dictates of civilization. We are driven creatures who create our own suffering through the clash between our asocial, somatically based sexual and aggressive fantasies and drives and the constricting and repressive demands of

civilization. A life without tension is as good as it gets. Human suffering, according to Freud and most subsequent psychoanalysts, can be lessened although not eliminated. In a world in which suffering cannot be eradicated, the good life involves the capacity to approach life with clear-eyed rationality; to peel away distorting illusions including erroneous religious hopes for salvation; to bear life's burdens with greater clarity and stoical equanimity; and to love and work with a measure of success and fulfillment. Psychoanalysis tends to debunk what is positive in the search for the hidden and seamy underside of apparently constructive ideals and behavior. Is it any wonder psychoanalysts and psychotherapists (to borrow from Shakespeare), "know what we are but not what we may be?"

Psychoanalysis and the Good Life

The examined life is, for Freud, essential to the good life. Freud continued and radically extended the centuries-old Augustinian tradition of deep self-investigation with his writings on the unconscious and transference, resistance and dreamwork. Since Freud plumbed the unconscious, human reflection, action, and morality have been greatly complicated. The unconscious is another word for the ubiquity of self-deception, the impossibility of complete self-awareness, and the possibility of exquisite creativeness. We are not transparent to ourselves. Actions and intentions have multiple conscious and unconscious meanings and functions. There are at least four morals to this story: In such a world (1) we can never completely know ourselves; (2) we have an endless capacity to deceive ourselves; (3) we have an exquisite capacity for unconsciously communicating with ourselves and healing ourselves; and (4) the examined life is never-ending.

"Turn your eyes inward," writes Freud (1917), "look into your own depths, learn first to know yourself." A central assumption of Buddhism is that without formal training—like meditation—most people sleepwalk through life, unaware of the actual texture of their experience. Without a regular meditative practice, we are more prone to get emotionally highjacked by thoughts, feelings, and fantasies. We plan and obsess, daydream and worry. We tend to endlessly rehash the past and anticipate the future. Meanwhile we miss the present.

Participating in therapy, on-going self-analysis, and supervision obviously cultivates greater self-awareness. Buddhism also recommends another technique, namely meditation—attending to our experience with a spirit of self-friendship, that is, with curiosity and acceptance.

The Vietnamese Zen teacher Thich Nhat Hanh gives a daily life example of mindfulness:

> While washing the dishes you might be thinking about the tea afterward, and so try to get them [the dishes] out of the way as quickly as possible in order to drink the tea. But that means that you are incapable of living

during the time you are washing the dishes. When you are washing the dishes, washing the dishes must be the most important thing in your life. Just as when you are drinking tea, drinking tea must be the most important thing in your life (Thich Nhat Hanh, 1987).

Meditation is an incomparable means of cultivating moment-to-moment awareness or attentiveness. A Zen story illustrates the way the mindfulness Buddhism points toward is more extensive than what we ordinarily mean when we think or talk about awareness.

> Nan-in [a teacher of Zen] was visited by Tenno, [a student and aspiring teacher of Zen] who, having passed his apprenticeship [to teach], had become a teacher. The day happened to be rainy, so Tenno wore wooden clogs and carried an umbrella. After greeting him Nan-in remarked: 'I suppose you left your wooden clogs in the vestibule. I want to know if your umbrella is on the right or left side of the clogs?' Tenno, confused, had no instant answer. He realized that he was unable to carry his Zen every minute. He became Nan-in's pupil, and he studied six more years to accomplish his every-minute Zen (Reps, 1989).

Meditation cultivates the capacity to hear when we listen, see when we look, and taste when we eat. Formerly inaccessible thoughts, feelings, and fantasies emerge. We develop the capacity to sit with and through a wider range of feelings. Our tolerance for the different facets of our experience expands. We become more self-accepting. We also become more present. We can more easily deeply commune with ourselves, other people, animals, and nature. Empathy and compassion are deeply cultivated (Rubin, 1996).

Our culture is permeated with the implicit as well as explicit search to transcend the dizzying complexity of inner life and embodied existence. The notion of the unconscious casts severe doubt on the dream of self-mastery and self-transcendence. When complete self-awareness is viewed as an illusion, as it is within psychoanalysis, the examined life is seen as never-ending. Mental health and the good life are then seen as a process not a destination. Melanie Klein (1960/1975) pointed to the irreducibly fluid nature of mental life; the way, that is, that we experience alternating states of being each with their own particular styles of relatedness and defensiveness. Mental health, from this Kleinian perspective, involves skillfully navigating the ever-changing and sometimes turbulent waters of our lives without drowning, rather than transcending difficulties forever and reaching a perfect, static, conflict-free state of being.

"How sad that people ignore the near/And search for truth afar…" writes Hakuin (1685–1768) in "Song of Zazen": "Truly, is anything missing now?/ Nirvana is right here, before our eyes…" In Japanese aesthetics there is a great emphasis on "wabi-sabi," sometimes translated as the "beauty" of things "imperfect" and "incomplete" (Koren, 1994). Eschewing the illusory ideals of perfection that permeate our culture, psychoanalysis joins Japanese aesthetics and Zen in a this-(rather than other)-worldly conception of living, which provides a realistic ideal as well as tempers the quick fix mentality that reigns in our culture. The implication is that the good life entails engaging and embracing life moment-to-moment in its messiness and complexity rather than striving to achieve a permanent and irreversible state of health that is beyond and devoid of suffering and conflict.

People demand it and forfeit it; seek it and lose it; what is this desideratum we call freedom? Freedom demands continual attentiveness. The examined life is interminable.

Freedom is often talked about in contemporary popular and academic discourse in polarized terms: we are free or we are determined; we are puppets of language and history, according to postmodernists, or we are capable of "just saying no;" "just doing it," as self-help gurus claim. The work of Freud in particular and psychoanalysis in general suggests that the terms of these debates are problematic because they polarize what are mutually interconnected and reinforcing experiences of being; namely being determined and having the capacity for reflection and self-transformation. Freedom for Freud was always contextual and relative never absolute: what I think of as a practitioner of martial arts—who continually experiences the reality of physical constraints—as a freedom-within-structure. While we are all authors of our own lives, our authorship is not without limitations. We are also determined. One can never transcend what Shakespeare termed "the ten thousand shocks that flesh is heir to" but one can gain a measure of freedom. This is what Peter Gay (1990), in a felicitous phrase, terms Freud's "deterministic psychology of freedom."

For Ferenczi the possibilities for freedom were more radical than for Freud: it was possible not only to experience mental health, but to lead a more unfettered life. In his reflections on dissolving transference and super-ego formations and living in a liberated way in "The Elasticity of Psychoanalytic Technique" (1928/1980) there are intimations of the freedom that he believed psychoanalysis at its best could foster:

> it is the business of a real character analysis to do away, at any rate temporarily, with any kind of super-ego, including that of the analyst. The patient should end by ridding himself of any emotional attachment that is independent of his own reason and his own libidinal tendencies. Only a complete dissolution of the super-ego can bring about a radical cure. Successes that consist in the substitution of one super-ego for another must be regarded as transference successes; they fail to attain the final aim of therapy, the dissolution of the transference...The ideal result of a completed analysis is precisely that elasticity which analytic technique demands of the mental therapist.

The good life, for Ferenczi, was the uncoerced and liberated life. We don't free associate in order to be cured, he (1927/1980) writes, we are cured when we can free associate, by which I think he meant, living with greater playful-ness and freedom, authenticity and spontaneity rather than social conformity, automatic compliance, or self-neglectful responsibility for others.

With freedom comes responsibility. Contemporary popular and academic discussions of suffering, evil, and ethics tend to establish false contrasts: splitting moral accountability and empathy. Right-wing political commenta-tors tend to demand moral accountability but are not empathic toward the poverty-stricken or oppressed. Liberal apologists for the downtrodden express empathy for their plight but sometimes neglect their contribution to it.

At its best, psychoanalysis encourages empathic understanding of the experience of the oppressed or oppressor, while also acknowledging moral responsibility. "Moral responsibility," for Loewald (1978), involves "appropri-ating" one's history, by which he means, reworking, reorganizing, and trans-forming our sense of our past so as to create a unique life in the present. This involves integrating and drawing on our histories rather than being excessively detached from or driven by them. If we are either too disengaged from our past or entangled in it, then our lives are depleted and enslaved, respectively. We are then not morally responsible in the present. For Loewald, human life is devitalized if we neglect our past, which is the potential wellspring of our life in the present; the root of our sense of ourselves and the world, our mean-ings and our passions. Our past experiences—even negative ones—are like manure that fertilize the garden of our lives; adding depth and texture to the way we live in the present. The past is defensively evaded when psychospir-itual traditions treat only the present as real and the past as illusory and coun-sel spiritual seekers to "let go" of it. Many spiritual seekers strive to become detached from painful experiences from their past rather than engaging and integrating them into their lives in the present. The past is also neglected when popular self-help writings recommend that we "just get over" our past.

If we voluntarily sever links with our past, we create a discontinuous sense of our own history which makes us feel adrift and devitalized in the present. And we are then condemned, as Santayana warned, to repeat our history and thereby impoverish our life in the present. I suspect that this is one reason some meditators struggle with the same conflicts over self-care and intimacy even after years of meditating.

The person who avoids their emotional life by, let us say, minimizing or repressing losses or trauma through cultivating detachment may well become at the mercy of the feelings they have disowned. I am thinking of a Buddhist who suffered traumatic losses as an adolescent and trained himself to detach from painful feelings. After college he began meditating and refined his capacity to disavow disturbing emotions. He denied his pain, never mourned his losses, adopted a super-independent stance toward life, and avoided pain-ful arenas of life including dependence on others for emotional sustenance. The losses that were disavowed still haunted and impoverished his life years later. As an adult he had little intimacy and less loss. He avoided whole facets of life that threatened to trigger feelings and deep anguish. His capacity for intimacy and for empathizing with the emotional pain of others, for example, was deeply compromised.

If we are too immersed in the past—haunted by old memories and experiences—then time is repetitious and narrow, and we betray the present. The aliveness of the present is deeply diminished as we accommodate it to old scenarios and expectations.

When we are too engrossed or attached to our past or our emotional experience then we are prone to being hyperreactive and unreflective. We have no panoramic perspective on our experience or our lives, which sometime resemble an emotional roller-coaster. Our submersion in our own subjectivity also compromises our relationships with other people. We view them egocentrically—only in terms of how they affect us—rather than as separate beings with their own unique values, wishes, and needs. Our relationships are then more conflictual and disappointing.

Appropriating our history, in Loewald's view, entails drawing on our experience as a crucial resource for our subsequent life rather than either getting lost in or evading it. The past is not so much outgrown, according to Loewald, but woven into our current life. An important aspect of appropriating our histories involves what I have termed "self-creation" in the present (Rubin, 1998). Self-creation refers to building a personally authentic and meaningful life in the present by creatively reworking and transforming ourselves. When we draw upon the experience and meanings embodied in our history but are not subsumed by them, our lives in the present have greater meaning and richness. Such a life is neither a sterile imitation of another's existence, nor a reactive rebellion against ways of living that we may in fact value, but a life that has texture, vitality, and depth and feels creative and alive and authentically one's own (Rubin, 2011). Unsuspected ways of relating to ourselves and others emerge.

But ordinarily such moral accountability, like freedom, is elusive. We are usually quite attached to our sense of ourselves and our view of the world, which makes us rigid. We want the world and our lives to unfold according to our vision of it. When life does not conform to our expectations we are frustrated and angry. Buddhists might argue that such attachment—by which they mean something very different than psychoanalysts—not money, is the real root of all evil. For this kind of attachment leads to an excessively self-centered perspective. It makes us place ourselves at the center of the universe and we become selfish and greedy. It causes us to be less kindhearted and less open to the uniqueness and difference of others, which fosters emotional and intellectual intolerance.

Attachment in psychoanalytic circles takes various forms including thinking that the theories we believe in or the analytic school of thought that we identify with is the only valid one; leading to denigrating therapists who have different beliefs and allegiances. When challenged we get defensive instead of curious about what another viewpoint might teach us. What Buddhism terms nonattachment, or a non-clinging and non-possessive relationship to ourselves, other people, and the world, is central to freedom, compassion, and wisdom.

A story from the Zen tradition illustrates what Buddhism means by attachment and non-attachment. Two Zen monks, Tanzan and Ekido, were once traveling together down a muddy road. A heavy rain was still falling. Coming around a bend, they met a lovely girl in a silk kimono and sash, unable to cross the intersection. "Come on, girl" said Tanzan at once. Lifting her in his arms, he carried her over the mud. Ekido [the other Zen monk] did not speak again until that night when they reached a lodging temple. Then he longer could restrain himself. "We monks don't go near females," he told Tanzan, "especially not young and lovely ones. It is dangerous. Why did you do that?" "I left the girl there," said Tanzan. "Are you still carrying her?" (Reps, 1989).

Engaging the world not renouncing it, is essential in the best of psychoanalysis and Buddhism. There are periodic warnings in Buddhism about the dangers of detachment. There was an old woman in China who had supported a monk for over twenty years. She had built a little hut for him and fed him while he was meditating. Finally, she wondered what progress he had made. To find out, she obtained the help of a girl rich in desire. "Go and embrace him," she told her, "and then suddenly ask: What now?" The girl called upon the monk and without much ado caressed him, asking him what he was going to do about it. "An old tree grows on a cold rock in winter," replied the monk somewhat poetically. "Nowhere is there any warmth." The girl returned and related what he had said [to the old woman].

"To think I fed that fellow for twenty years!" exclaimed the old woman in anger. "He showed no consideration for your need, no disposition to explain your condition. He need not have responded to passion, but at least he should have evidenced some compassion." "She at once went to the hut of the monk and burned it down" (Reps, 1989).

An ethos of asceticism, renunciation, and melancholia haunts psychoanalysis as well as Buddhism. Assuming that mental health involves a stoical life of clear-eyed rationality without illusions, many psychoanalysts since Freud, tacitly or explicitly counsel renouncing, foregoing, or abstaining from unrealistic or illusory desires and wishes. That this "appetite lost" (Phillips, 1998) may breed a somber and melancholic spirit seems insufficiently discussed in psychoanalysis.

If "appetite lost" is a central facet of the classical psychoanalytic vision of the good life, then "appetite regained" (Phillips, 1998) is crucial to what I would provisionally term the "aestheticist" wing of post-classical psychoanalysis. The heroic, individuated artist, striving for authentic self-expression and self-transcendence, not the somber, stoical rationalist, embodied for Winnicott as it did years before for Otto Rank, the good life. There is more to life than confronting our fate with clarity and dignity, according to Rank. We could also create something enduring—through contributing to one's community, raising a happy child, or fashioning a work of art—that might outlast us and thus grant us the opportunity to go beyond ourselves and perhaps transcend our tragic fate. This, for Rank, is essential to a well-lived life. The good life, for contemporary analysts along this aestheticist axis such as Phillips, involves curiosity, exuberance, and ecstasy

Freud's work on the unconscious and dream-work offers an unsuspected doorway into the enriching universe of "appetite regained." There is a deep human predilection to reduce; to narrow down the mysterious and won-drous abundance that we call life. "Newton's vision and single sleep," Blake (Erdman, 1988) terms it. We search for our essence, speculate about our des-tiny. It is reassuring. It creates an apparent order; a world that can be mapped. Emily Dickinson (1957) wrote: "The Soul selects her own society/then shuts the door/On her divine majority/Obtrude no more... I've known her from an ample nation/Choose one/Then close the valves of her attention." The nature of dream-work—particularly its dense complexity and its idiosyncratic mean-ing and nature—suggests that we are all (even the most prosaic among us) artists; capable of creating fertile, unique, and often surreal, dreamscapes that capture with brilliant lucidity and specificity our hopes and fears, our demons and our saviors.

The dreaming experience is not something that happens only when we are asleep. "Oh, these humans of old knew how to dream and did not need to fall asleep first," wrote Nietzsche (quoted in Duerr, 1985). The dreaming mode of thinking—the creation of condensed and displaced symbols and images related to unfinished feelings, fantasies, and conflicts from our past that are triggered by experiences in the present that are imbued with unsuspected meanings—happens when we are awake as a backdrop to our conscious thinking and feeling.

The dreaming experience—and the uniquely creative way that Freud, Jung, and Ullman, among others, taught us to play with dreams—is appli-cable to daily life. If we take the dream as a model for the unconscious operation of thought; and free association and evenly hovering attention as potentially creative ways of speaking and listening that encourage uncon-scious facets of our experience to emerge—as Bollas (1992) does—then we would experience our emotional life and the world in a more fertile and creative way. One of my supervisors in psychoanalytic training illus-trated this when he encouraged me to listen to intellectual discourse and everyday speech, no less than patients, with that meditative state of mind Freud (1912) termed "evenly hovering attention" (Henry Lothane, personal communication). Then the world of daily life—sights and sounds, images and ideas in novels or movies, the art in our homes and offices, the people we converse with, the plays and music that move us, and the sensuous pleasures we relish—are potentially pregnant with unsuspected meanings. Overdetermined, emotionally charged, condensed and displaced images that symbolically encode unresolved emotional conflicts and unrealized potentials from the past are evoked by these and other experiences in the present in what Bollas (1992), in a felicitous phrase, terms the "dream work of one's life." As we develop the capacity to play with and associate to these images in an uncensored and unfettered way, a variety of further meanings emerge and point in unpredictable directions. New insights, questions, pathways, and dreams are generated by our secondary process reflection upon and interpretation of these evocative trains of thought and emotion. Our internal creativity may lie fallow for a while until an experience in the present triggers new condensed and displaced images resplendent with evocative possibilities, which we then decode. And so on and so on.

The external environment, as well as our emotional life, can be reanimated when we are attuned to the dream work of our lives. How we experience the world is shaped, in no small measure, by how we look. Winnicott taught us that a child's torn blanket was, for an imaginative toddler, not a worthless and disposable item, but a precious possession.

A teenager asks his mother to drive to the back of a small shopping center near where they live. When they arrive at the back of the mini mall he is overjoyed while she is perplexed. Because she only "sees" debris—garbage cans from the restaurants and stores, worn stairs and chipped rails—she cannot fathom why he wanted to go there and why he is so happy. "You are not looking at this place as a skater would," he tells her. He has noticed that she has failed to recognize that the fire hydrant, staircase, and ledge were a heavenly course for an in-line skating and skateboarding enthusiast such as himself.

A unique perspective on the nature of the self, as well as moral responsibility, emerges when we are receptive to the dream work of our lives. Post-modern discourse recognizes the complexity of the self but then makes an unwarranted and erroneous epistemological leap and claims that our existence is illusory, a Lacanian mirage. Psycho-spiritual writings, however, herald the finding of an authentic, idealized, essential, selfless self. Contemporary popular culture offers a less "spiritual," but equally essentialist vision of the self. "You be you," Nike commercials beseech us. But are we singular? And do we have a particular destiny?

Seeing the self as like a dream, by which I mean, as a dense, complex, and unfinished and emergent phenomenon—a kind of work-of-art-in-progress—presents an illuminating perspective on self-experience. It also offers a critique of the nihilism of postmodern views and the essentialism of popular and spiritual conceptions of self.

In Western secular culture the self is often treated as the highest good and the desires of the isolated individual are worshiped, which fosters self-inflation and breeds narcissism. Narcissism is implicated in a great range of evil and is the source of immense suffering in our world. Self-centeredness is viewed as a villain according to Eastern meditative traditions, the cause of greed and immorality. Spiritual traditions celebrate the virtues of selflessness. While the spiritual sense of self opens up new possibilities for living, there are pathologies of spirit ranging from the "spiritual materialism" (Trungpa,1973) of contemplative seekers who use spiritual experiences as a mark of distinction; as a way of competing with and feeling better than others; to fusion experiences that lead to self-effacement not self-transcendence (Rubin, 2004).

But "regard for the self is not evil," Abraham Heschel (1955) reminds us. "It is when arrogating to the self what is not its due, enhancing one's interest at the expense of others or setting up the self as an ultimate goal that evil comes into being." I have repeatedly witnessed among meditators that I know and have treated the way Eastern contemplative viewpoints can breed self-neglect. This occurs when one uses meditation to detach from rather than engage one's troubling past and when one treats others as more important instead of equal to oneself (Rubin, 2004).

In the work of Fromm, Winnicott, and Kohut, among others, psychoanalysis suggests a third, more constructive option to the alienating hedonism of secular individualism and the self-nullifying predilection of renunciate spiritual doctrines. Altruism and self-care are both essential aspects of a balanced life, according to these and other psychoanalysts.

By highlighting our complexity and fluidity, contemporary relationally oriented analysts such as Mitchell, Hoffman, Eigen, Stolorow, Atwood, and Bromberg suggest that it is possible to recognize our multidimensionality without falling into the postmodernist fallacy of jettisoning our individuality. They also make us more skeptical about the singular, essentialist, and authentic self of contemplative and pop psycho-spiritual writings. A richer sense of human subjectivity is possible when we reflect upon the fluid, multidimensional, and unfinished self depicted in psychoanalytic writings. Intersubjectivists such as Stolorow, Brandchaft, and Atwood (1987), for example, describe the possibility of a life that is imbued with greater insight, self-stability, flexibility, affect tolerance, and more complex experiences of self. The self is then like a symphony orchestra with many instruments (rationality and passion, the capacity for will and yielding, insight and action) that need to play together in harmony (Rubin, 1996, 2011).

Jung radicalizes and enlarges psychoanalytic views of the self. For Jung, the field of what constitutes the well-lived life expands from the individual's self-realization and self-actualization to their relation to the universe, to what we might think of as a spiritual self or sense of the universe. There are, for Jung, at least three facets to the life well-lived: individuation (becoming our uniqueness), wholeness (integrating opposites—including male and female values and qualities—and becoming multidimensional beings), and living with a "religious attitude." Individuation involves the development of our uniqueness and our full humanity. The Jungian emphasis on the integration of opposites is very important because of what the Greeks and the Stoics termed *antakolouthia* or the "mutual entailment of the virtues" (Murphy, 1992). We ordinarily think of virtues as self-sufficient, complete, and, as it were, capable of standing on their own. But no virtue or quality—even apparently valuable ones such as honesty or awareness—is virtuous by itself. Honesty without compassion, for example, can be cruelty. Awareness devoid of action can remain merely intellectual knowledge. A well-lived life requires the balancing and integration of seeming opposites—altruism and self-care, insight and action, honesty and compassion.

The third crucial facet of a life well-lived for Jung is a "religious" attitude; realizing we are embedded in a larger lifeworld imbued with depth, sacredness, and meaning and approaching that world with reverence and scrupulous attentiveness.

Buddhism implicitly says that there is more to being a human being than becoming an integrated and cohesive self, which is the acme of mental health in psychoanalysis. Buddhism views this psychoanalytic achievement as an arrested, sub-optimal state of development. For contemplatives, to be fully human is to move beyond the psychoanalytic and common-sense belief that one's life is the ultimate value. Buddhism implicitly points to a vital and neglected facet of self-experience, what I have termed the non-self-centered or spiritual self, by which I mean a non-self-preoccupied state of being in which one is open to the moment without a sense of time, un-self-conscious but acutely aware, self-forgetful yet not self-neglectful, highly focused and engaged although relaxed and without fear (Rubin, 1996, 1998, 2004). Many of us have had such experiences—perhaps communing with nature or a loved one, meditating or praying, playing sports or creating art.

Since Buddhism speaks of the illusoriness of the autonomous, self-identical, independent self, this way of thinking about self-experience might be objectionable. Buddhism's critique of our taken-for-granted sense of self usefully highlights the transitory nature of consciousness and self-experience. But in highlighting the fluid nature of mind it neglects its substantial, historical nature and the recurrent patterns of thought and action that shape our character and our experience of self and relationships. One of the hallmarks of Taoism, which was central to the origin of Zen, was the inextricable interconnection of apparent opposites—you can't have high without low, large without small and so forth. Ironically, when Buddhism focuses on one side of an interrelated pair of opposites—impermanence—while neglecting its other side (continuity) it ignores its own Taoist roots. The non-self-centered self is my own attempt to preserve the germ of truth in Buddhist formulations without subscribing to its problematic facets.

Compassion is a crucial ingredient of a life well-lived, according to Buddhism. Psychoanalysts such as Fromm and Kohut have emphasized empathy, concern, and compassion as well as authenticity, self-realization, and creativity as important facets of the live well-lived. Buddhism expands and enriches how we conceive of compassion. It implicitly suggests that psychoanalysis has underestimated human possibilities in this area. The compassion Buddhism points to is more than empathy—the ability to enter into and share another's suffering. In dissolving the barriers between self and other, the non-self-centered self makes possible a different kind of consciousness of self in relation to others. When self-experience is less self-referential and self-preoccupied we feel more connected to people and to nature. We can then ask: not "what did the other do (or not do) for the self?"—the question we usually focus on in psychoanalysis and daily life—but rather, "what might the self do for the other?"

Cultivating the experience of non-separation and intimacy towards all people, including those who may wish to harm us, leads to what Tibetan Buddhists term "great compassion" (Gyatso, 1999). This widens the circle of compassion to include all living beings not simply those closest to us. Morality can be viewed in more universalist and less exclusive ways because of the concern for the other as well as the self. This fosters a radical sense of responsibility towards others which includes ethical conduct toward strangers and the environment as well as family and friends.

I have highlighted several key dimensions of a life well-lived within psychoanalytic and Buddhist writings ranging from self-awareness to interpersonal attunement to universal compassion. What are some of the morals of the tales psychoanalysis and Buddhism tell about a live well-lived? The good life is protean rather than standard brand. There is no single best way of living. Each person must discover and create how they want to live rather than accommodate to anyone else's version including their psychoanalyst or Buddhist teacher. Since inner experience is fluid rather than static, this changes moment-to-moment. Health involves engaging life with care and attentiveness in all its complexity rather than attempting to transcend the struggles that we all must contend with. Living a good life resembles skillfully riding the ever-changing waves of our experience rather than arriving at a pre-ordained endpoint. Part of leading a full life entails operating on all cylinders rather than perfecting partial domains. This self-multidimensionality requires integrating and balancing complementary qualities such as awareness and moral action and rationality and ecstasy, rather than cultivating particular isolated virtues. One needs to strive to be free even as one must continually confront how one is determined. The good life entails attunement to the other as well as cultivation of the self. Living with compassion and empathy as well as authenticity and vitality, are crucial to this process.

Dancing in the spaces between psychoanalysis and Buddhism and fostering a cross-pollinating dialogue between these two wisdom traditions might greatly enrich the quality of our lives and aid us in experiencing a well-lived life.

References

Auden, Wystan Hugh. *The Dyer's Hand, and Other Essays*. New York: Random House, 1962.

Bollas, Christopher. *Being a Character: Psychoanalysis and Self Experience*. New York: Hill and Wang, 1992. Page 53.

Breger, Louis. *Freud's Unfinished Journey: Conventional and Critical Perspectives*. London: Hogarth, 1981.

Breuer, Josef, and Sigmund Freud. *Studies on Hysteria. The Standard Edition*, Standard Edition, 2. London: Hogarth Press, 1895.

Dickinson, Emily. *Poems*. Boston: Little, Brown & Company, 1957. Page 9.

Duerr, Hans Peter. *Dreamtime: Concerning the Boundary Between Wilderness and Civilization*. Oxford: Basil Blackwell, 1985. Page 114.

Erdman, David, ed. *The Complete Poetry and Prose of William Blake*. New York: Anchor Books, 1988. Page 722.

Farber, Leslie. *Lying, Despair, Jealousy, Envy, Sex, Suicide, Drugs, and the Good Life*. New York: Basic Books, 1976.

Ferenczi, Sandor. "The Problem of the Termination of the Analysis." In *Final Contributions to the Problems and Methods of Psycho-Analysis*. New York: Brunner/Mazel, 1927/1980. Pages 77–86.

Ferenczi, Sandor. "The Elasticity of Psychoanalytic Technique." In *Final Contributions to the Problems and Methods of Psycho-Analysis*. New York: Brunner/Mazel, 1928/1980. Pages 87–101.

Freud, Sigmund. *Recommendations to Physicians Practicing Psycho-Analysis, The Standard Edition*, 12. London: Hogarth Press, 1912. Pages 109–120, 304.

Freud, Sigmund. *A Difficulty in the Path of Psycho-Analysis, The Standard Edition*, 17. London: Hogarth Press, 1917. Pages 135–144, 142f.

Fromm, Erich. *Man for Himself*. New York: Henry Holt and Company, 1947. Page 17.

Fromm, Erich. *The Essential Erich Fromm*. New York: Continuum, 1995.

Gay, Peter. "Freud and Freedom." In *Reading Freud: Explorations and Entertainments*. New Haven: Yale University Press, 1990. Pages 74–94.

Gyatso, Tenzin. *Ethics for the New Millennium*. New York: Riverhead Books, 1999. Pages 9, 124.

Hanh, Thich. *The Miracle of Mindfulness*. Boston: Beacon Press, 1987. Page 24.

Heschel, Abraham. *God in Search of Man: A Philosophy of Judaism*. New York: Farrar, Straus and Giroux, 1955. Page 400.

Klein, Melanie. "On Mental Health." In *Envy and Gratitude and Other Works (1946–1963)*. New York: Dell, 1960/1975. Pages 176–235.

Koren, Leonard. *Wabi-Sabi for Artists, Designers, Poets and Philosophers*. Berkeley, CA: Stone Bridge Press, 1994. Page 7.

Loewald, Hans. *Psychoanalysis and the History of the Individual*. New Haven: Yale University Press, 1978. Page 8.

Molino, Anthony, and Christine Ware, eds. *Where Id Was: Challenging Normalization in Psychoanalysis*. New York: Continuum, 2001.

Murphy, Michael. *The Future of the Body*. Los Angeles: Tarcher, 1992.

Novick, Jack. Termination Conceivable and Inconceivable. *Psychoanalytic Psychology*. 14, 1997. Pages 145–162.

Phillips, Adam. *The Beast in the Nursery*. New York: Pantheon Books, 1998.

Reps, Paul, ed. *Zen Flesh Zen Bones: A Collection of Zen and Pre-Zen Writings*. New York: Anchor Doubleday Books, 1989. Pages 18, 34, 10.

Rubin, Jeffrey B. *Psychotherapy and Buddhism: Toward an Integration*. New York: Plenum Press, 1996.

Rubin, Jeffrey B. *A Psychoanalysis for Our Time: Exploring the Blindness of the Seeing I*. New York: New York University Press, 1998.

Rubin, Jeffrey B. *The Good Life: Psychoanalytic Reflections on Love, Ethics, Creativity, and Spirituality*. Albany, NY: State University of New York Press, 2004.

Rubin, Jeffrey B. *The Art of Flourishing: A New East-West Approach to Staying Sane and Finding Love in an Insane World*. New York: Random House, 2011.

Schafer, Roy. *A New Language for Psychoanalysis*. New Haven: Yale University Press, 1976.

Stolorow, Robert, Bernard Brandchaft, and George Atwood. *Psychoanalytic Treatment: An Intersubjective Approach*. Hillsdale, NJ: The Analytic Press, 1987.

Trungpa, Chögyam. *Cutting Through Spiritual Materialism*. Boston: Shambhala, 1973.

Wallwork, Ernest. "A Constructive Alternative to Psychotherapeutic Egoism." In *Community in America: The Challenges of Habits of the Heart,* edited by Charles Reynolds and Ralph Norman. Berkeley, CA: University of California Press, 1988. Pages 202–214.

Winnicott, Donald W. *Playing and Reality*. London: Tavistock Publications, 1971. Page 98.

Part IV

Recommended Resources

Writing

Atwood, George. *The Abyss of Madness*. London: Routledge, 2012.

This collection of case studies by an extraordinary clinician, display a rare clinical acumen and shed light on a range of topics including depression and dreams, suicidiality and schizophrenia.

Buddha. "Mahāsatipatthāna Sutta: The Greater Discourse on the Foundations of Mindfulness." In *Thus Have I Heard: The Long Discourses of the Buddha*. London: Wisdom Publications, 1987. Pages 335–350.

The Mahāsatipatthāna Sutra is the classic Buddhist description of how to meditate, focusing on mindfulness in every aspect of our lives.

Freud, Sigmund. "The Dream Work and the Primary and Secondary Process." In *The Interpretation of Dreams. Standard Edition*, 5. London: Hogarth Press, 1900. Pages 599–609; 277–281; 305–309.

Freud's exploration of the unconscious mind, the dream work, and the primary and secondary processes remains a central text in psychoanalytic theory, offering a powerful framework for understanding the unconscious mechanisms behind dreams and the psychology of everyday life.

Freud, Sigmund. "Recommendations to Physicians on Practicing Psycho-Analysis." In *Standard Edition*, 12. London: Hogarth Press, 1912. Pages 111–120.

Freud describes: the ideal therapist's state of mind to listen, emphasizing "evenly hovering attention," as well as unconscious attunement and communication, which remain essential concepts in psychoanalytic practice and our ordinary lives.

Friedman, Lenore. *Meetings with Remarkable Women: Buddhist Teachers in America*. Boston: Shambhala, 2000.

This book celebrates remarkable women teaching Buddhism in America. Through interviews with seventeen visionary teachers—including but not limited to—Sharon Salzberg and Pema Chodron, Joko Beck and Toni Packer, Maurine Stuart and Ruth Denison, the reader gains greater insight into Buddhism, American culture, and themselves.

Goldstein, Joseph. *Mindfulness: A Practical Guide to Awakening*. Boulder, CO: Sounds True, 2016.

One of America's most respected teachers gives a guided tour of the *Mahāsatipatthāna Sutta,* the Buddha's legendary discourse on the four foundations of mindfulness. Drawing on five decades of teaching and practice, he illuminates how Vipassana (or insight meditation) can enrich our lives in undreamt of ways.

Goldstein, Joseph, *One Dharma: The Emerging Western Buddhism*. San Francisco: Harper, 2002. Not only a visionary synthesis of the essential and invaluable facets of each school of Western Buddhism, but a nonsectarian blending in which differences among and between traditions are viewed as both integrable and as skillful means for liberation.

Goleman, Daniel. *The Meditative Mind: Varieties of the Meditative Experience*. Los Angeles: Jeremy Tarcher, 1988.

This book provides a comprehensive and accessible overview of several types of meditation, examining how meditation impacts the mind and can lead to emotional and spiritual growth.

Kohut, Heinz. "Introspection, Empathy, and Psychoanalysis." In: *The Search for the Self*, Vol. 1, edited by Paul Ornstein. New York: International Universities Press, 1978.

Kohut considered empathy ("vicarious introspection")—viewing the patient from within their own frame of reference—as the basic observational tool of psychoanalysis and the foundation for all of his work. The radical methodological revolution he ushered in was of immense value in the creation of meditative psychoanalysis.

Kornfield, Jack. *Living Buddhist Masters*. Santa Cruz, CA: Unity Press, 1977.

Interviews with and teachings of twelve highly respected masters from Southeast Asia including Mahasi Sayadaw and Achaan Jumnien, U Ba Khin and Achaan Buddhadasa. A lucid introduction by Kornfield, one of America's preeminent teachers, also sheds light on foundational teachings of Buddhism.

Kornfield, Jack. *A Path with Heart: A Guide Through the Perils and Promises of Spiritual Life*. New York: Bantam, 1993.

This book illuminates the challenges of spiritual living in the modern world—from addiction and psychological and emotional healing to relationships and creating balance in one's ordinary life.

Kornfield, Jack. *The Wise Heart: A Guide to the Universal Teachings of Buddhist Psychology*. New York: Bantam/Dell, 2008.

A clear and illuminating guide to Buddhism's transformational psychology including the nobility of the human spirit, a fine-grained examination of thought and emotion, and precise techniques for training and healing the mind and heart.

Kornfield, Jack. *Bringing Home the Dharma; Awakening Right Where You Are*. Boston: Shambhala, 2012.

This book reveals how your life as it is can be the arena in which you find peace and wisdom. Topics include conscious parenting, spirituality and sexuality, and forgiveness.

Nordstrom, Lou, ed. *Namu Dai Bosa: A Transmission of Zen Buddhism to America*. New York: The Zen Studies Society, 1976.

This collection of primary source writings from 20th-century Zen masters presents some of the most important teachings on Zen Buddhism, offering insight into its transmission and adaptation in America.

Rahula, Walpola. *What the Buddha Taught*. New York: Grove Press, 1959.
    A comprehensive, reliable, and accessible study of the essentials of Buddhism.

Rubin, Jeffrey B. *Psychotherapy and Buddhism: Toward an Integration*. New York: Plenum Press, 1996.

Rubin describes how psychotherapy and meditation can mutually enrich each other, offering clinical examples that demonstrate how these practices can be integrated effectively in therapeutic contexts.

Rubin, Jeffrey B. *The Art of Flourishing*. New York: Crown, 2011.

Rubin explores how to integrate meditative therapy into one's life to create more mean-
ing, intimacy, and fulfillment, offering practical advice for applying these principles.
Sayadaw, Mahasi. *Practical Insight Meditation*. Buddhist Publication Society, 1991.
Lucid description of the practice of Vipassana or insight meditation by a venerable
twentieth century master.
Schmidt, Amy. *Dipa Ma: The Life and Legacy of a Buddhist Master*. Katonah, New York:
BlueBridge, 2005.
The inspiring story of an extraordinary Buddhist teacher, Dipa Ma, who taught meditation and mindfulness amid the tumult of everyday life in her simple apartment in
Calcutta. She had a remarkable influence on her students, who included some of
the preeminent teachers of Buddhism in our time. Her profound compassion and
wisdom touched the hearts of countless spiritual seekers. She taught her students
how to embrace all circumstances so that every aspect of life can be a teacher. With
a heart open to all, she guided her students to reach beyond what they thought was
possible.
Stolorow, Robert. *Trauma and Human Existence*. New York: The Analytic Press, 2007.
This book is a fascinating and deeply personal illumination of the context-dependence
of emotional trauma and the profound importance of deep bonds of emotional
attunement—what he terms "kinship-in-the-same-darkness"—for healing.
Stolorow, Robert, and Atwood, George. *Contexts of Being: The Intersubjective Foundations of Psychological Life*. Hillsdale, NJ: The Analytic Press, 1992.
A lucid presentation of intersubjectivity theory, Stolorow and Atwood's seminal
post-Kohutian reformulation of psychoanalytic theory and practice. *Contexts of
Being* critiques a foundational facet of psychoanalysis—the Cartesian myth of the
isolated mind. It also reframes central assumptions of analytic theory—from the
unconscious to trauma along intersubjective lines, which played a significant role
in the creation of meditative psychoanalysis.
Suzuki, Shunryu. *Zen Mind, Beginner's Mind*. New York: Weatherhill, 1970.
A classic on meditation by a beloved Zen master that illuminates maintaining an
open and receptive approach to life—beginner's mind—and living wisely and
unself-consciously.
Young, Shinzen. *Break Through Pain*. Boulder, CO: Sounds True, 2004.
Young provides a clear and valuable exploration of how meditation can be used to
address both physical and emotional pain, guiding readers toward healing and
self-awareness.
Young, Shinzen. *What Is Meditation?* Reprint from Shinzen.org.
This concise and substantive description of meditation clarifies the essence of the
practice, providing readers with foundational knowledge of what meditation is.
Young, Shinzen. *Why Practice Mindfulness?* Reprint from Shinzen.org.
Young offers a thoughtful account of the value of mindfulness meditation, discussing
how it can enhance well-being, awareness, and emotional balance.
Young, Shinzen. *Five Ways to Know Yourself: An Introduction to Basic Mindfulness*.
Reprint from Shinzen.org.
This article presents an original and integrative approach to mindfulness, providing
readers with a comprehensive understanding of diverse ways of practicing.
Young, Shinzen. *The Science of Enlightenment*. Boulder, CO: Sounds True Adult, 2018.
A magisterial work by a visionary teacher blending scientific rigor, scholarly exper-
tise with Asian languages (Pali, Sanskrit, Chinese, and Tibetan), and comprehensive
knowledge of the full spectrum of meditative practices. A lucid guide to meditation
for beginners and seasoned practitioners alike.

Meditation Training Centers

Barre Center for Buddhist Studies, 149 Lockwood Road, Barre, MA 01005; (978) 355–2347; contact@buddhistinquiry.org

Vipassana

Vipassana Support International, 3330 Hannibal Road, Burlington, Ontario, Canada L 7M 1R7; Toll-free phone (866) 666–0874; Fax: (613) 968-2542; e-mail: vsiretreat@ gmail.com

Insight Meditation Society, 1230 Pleasant Street, Barre, MA 01005; www.dharma.org

Spirit Rock Meditation Center, P.O. Box 169, Woodacre, CA 94973; (415) 488–0164; www.spiritrock.org

Insight LA, PO Box 7278, Santa Monica, CA 90406

New York Insight, 115 West 29th Street - 12th floor, New York, NY 10001; www.imc.org

Tibetan

Dawn Mountain Tibetan Temple, 2726 Bissonnet Street, #240-415, Houston, TX 77005

Natural Dharma Fellowship, 253 Philbrick Hill Road, Springfield, NH 03284

Tibetan Buddhist Learning Center; (908) 689–6080; 93 Angen Road, Washington New Jersey 07882.

Tara Mandala; PO Box 3040, Pagosa Springs, CO,81147; (970) 731–3711; tatamandala.org

Tergar International; tergar.org

Katog Choling Mountain Retreat Center, PO Box 158, Parthenon, AR 72666; (870) 446–2952; krcontact@katog.org

Samden Ling, PO Box 86083, PO 97286; infosamdenling.org

Copper Mountain Institute, 286 Ranchitos Road, Corrales, New Mexico; (505) 898–9592; coppermount.org

Padma Samye Ling, New York, jowozegyal@catskill.net; padmasambhava.org; (607) 865–8068.

Dudjom Tersar Yeshe Nyingpo Temple, 19 West 16th Street, New York, NY 10011; the fearlesswisdom@gmail.com; (212) 691–8523

Techen Chokhar Ling; contact@sakyacenterla.org; sakyacenterla.org

The Vajrapani Institute: PO Box 2130, Boulder Creek, CA, 95006; https://vajrapani.org

Tsechen Kunchab Ling; 12 Edmunds Lane, Walden, NY 12586; 1 (845) 778–0113; 1 (301) 906–3378; https://sakyatemple.org/

Zen

Berkeley Zen Center, 1931 Russell Street, Berkeley, CA 94703; (510) 845–2403; https://berkeleyzencenter.org.

Lakeland Zen Community, 3140 Troy Avenue, Lakeland, FL; lakelandzencommunity@ gmail.com

San Francisco Zen Center, 300 Page Street, San Francisco, CA 94102; (415) 863–3136; (415) 354–0360; https://www.sfzc.org

Village Zendo, 260 West Broadway, New York, NY 10013; info@villagezendo.org

Zen Mountain Monastery, Zen Mountain Monastery, 871 Plank Rd, PO Box 197, Mount Tremper, NY 12457; https://zmm.org

Index

For Product Safety Concerns and Information please contact our EU
representative GPSR@taylorandfrancis.com
Taylor & Francis Verlag GmbH, Kaufingerstraße 24, 80331 München, Germany

9 781032 982977